SYLLABUS OF
AMERICAN LITERATURE

THE UNIVERSITY OF CHICAGO PRESS, CHICAGO 37
Cambridge University Press, London, N.W. 1, England
W. J. Gage & Co., Limited, Toronto 2B, Canada

SYLLABUS OF
AMERICAN LITERATURE

By

WILLIAM T. HASTINGS

Professor of English, Brown University

THE UNIVERSITY OF CHICAGO PRESS
CHICAGO · ILLINOIS

PREFACE TO THE SECOND EDITION

The following *Syllabus* aims to present the essential facts in the history of American literature, with critical judgments of the chief authors and the more significant works. The outline form, which makes possible brevity and condensation, has also the advantage of bringing out clearly in a somewhat graphic way the relations of authors and groups. Within the chief period divisions classification by literary forms has been followed, and perhaps somewhat more stress than usual has been laid on the development of the various forms. Following the text are chronological tables of dates in American history and in English literature, and indexes of authors and of subjects.

In preparing the *Syllabus* the various current histories have been used freely. Particular acknowledgment is due the *Cambridge History of American Literature* in connection with the presentation of certain topics not adequately treated elsewhere. In general, the *Cambridge History* is the most comprehensive and detailed work in the field, and contains invaluable general and special bibliographies. Acknowledgment is also due to the general histories of American literature by Bronson, Cairns, Richardson, Trent, and Wendell. Use has been made also of the following works: Tyler's *History of American Literature, 1607–1676,* and *Literary History of the American Revolution,* Brownell's *American Prose Masters,* Trent and Erskine's *Great American Writers,* Pattee's *History of American Literature since 1870,* Van Doren's *American Novel,* Quinn's *Representative American Plays,* Miss Lowell's *Tendencies in Modern American Poetry,* and Untermeyer's *New Era in American Poetry.*

W. T. H.

PREFACE TO THE THIRD EDITION

Because of the continued demand for a brief but comprehensive survey of American Literature, it has seemed desirable to bring this *Syllabus* up to date.

In the difficult task of summarizing in brief compass the great literary activity of the last two decades I have been helped by the generalizations in Volume III of Parrington's *Main Currents in American Thought*, H. J. Muller's *Modern Fiction*, Anita Block's *Changing World in Plays and Theatre*, and Babette Deutsch's *This Modern Poetry*. Whether agreeing or disagreeing with them, I have profited also from the essays of many of the critics included in the *Syllabus*, as well as the host of named or unnamed reviewers in the *Times Literary Supplement*, the *Saturday Review of Literature*, and the *New York Times*. Thanks are due, too, to my colleagues, Professors Sharon Brown, Ben Brown, and Kapstein.

W. T. H.

TABLE OF CONTENTS

COLONIAL LITERATURE

1607-1765

I. The Background

A. Pioneer society, largely of the middle class, without much cultural interest and absorbed by the problems of social security and conquest of the wilderness.

B. Imaginative and aesthetic elements lacking in the writing of the period; virtually no genuine poetry, drama, or fiction.

II. Narratives, Diaries, and Other Historical Works

A. Narratives of the first settling, mainly by emigrants

   1. Virginia. Captain JOHN SMITH (1580?-1631), explorer and adventurer, leader in founding the Virginia colony, wrote *A True Relation of . . . . Occurrences . . . . in Virginia* (1608), "the first printed American book"; *A Description of New England* (1616); *The General History of Virginia, New England . . . .* (1624). Style vivid, with some Elizabethan exaggeration: truth of some incidents in doubt.

   2. New England

     a) First reports from Plymouth: "MOURT's" *Relation* (1622) and EDWARD WINSLOW's *Good News from New England* (1624).

     b) WILLIAM BRADFORD (1588-1657), in *The History of Plymouth Plantation* (completed 1650; published 1856), brought down the story to the year 1646. Style has the charm of direct simplicity; "a Puritan book in the best sense."

     c) JOHN WINTHROP (1588-1649), first governor of Massachusetts Bay Colony. His diary for the years 1630-49—published (1790) as *A Journal of the Transactions . . . . in the Settlement of Massachusetts . . . .* but usually, though inappropriately, called *The History of New England*—gives many intimate details of early Colonial life.

  d) THOMAS MORTON (died 1646), who defied the Puritans in
    his revels at "Merrymount," near Boston, and in his trading
    with the Indians, told his story and condemned the Puritans
    in his *New English Canaan* (1637).

  e) Captain EDWARD JOHNSON (died 1672) described with fervent
    but narrow enthusiasm the triumphs of the Puritans in the
    new land in his *Wonder-working Providence of Sion's Saviour
    in New England* (1654).

  f) NATHANIEL MORTON: *New England's Memorial* (1669),
    largely based upon the manuscript of Bradford's *History*.

B. Narratives dealing with the Indians

  1. Captain JOHN MASON's *Brief History of the Pequot War* (1677)
    is vivid but cold-blooded.

  2. Rev. WILLIAM HUBBARD's *Narrative of the Troubles with the
    Indians* (1677) and THOMAS CHURCH's *Entertaining Passages
    Relating to Philip's War* (1716) are somewhat undependable.

  3. MARY ROWLANDSON's *Narrative of the Captivity . . . .* (1682?)
    and JOHN WILLIAMS' *The Redeemed Captive* (1707) give moving
    accounts of the massacres by the Indians at Lancaster and
    Deerfield, Mass.

  4. [1]JOHN ELIOT,* translator of the Bible into the Indian tongue (1663),
    in *The Progress of the Gospel amongst the Indians in New-England*
    (1671), and DANIEL GOOKIN, in his *Historical Collections of the
    Indians in New England* (written 1674), present a view of the
    more friendly and humane contacts of the Puritans with the
    natives.

C. Diaries and journals

  1 SAMUEL SEWALL (1652–1730), a judge in the Salem witchcraft
    trials of 1692, but a kindly man of liberal views, friend of negroes
    and champion of women's rights. His *Diary*, for the years 1674–
    1729 (published 1878–82), gives a very intimate and detailed
    record of his private life, his wooings and marriages, love of
    funerals, dislike of wigs—and notes many important and trivial
    public happenings.

  [1]Authors whose names are marked with an asterisk appear in more than one
section of the *Syllabus*. See Index.

2. SARAH K. KNIGHT's *Journal of a Journey from Boston to New York in 1704* is very lively.

3. Colonel WILLIAM BYRD (1674–1744), a Virginian of the cavalier type, educated and cosmopolitan, witty and careless. Works left in manuscript (published 1841); have style and literary quality; represent the contrast between the spirit of the Northern and that of the Southern Colonies; include: *The History of the Dividing Line*, a journal of the expedition that surveyed the Virginia–North Carolina boundary; *A Journey to the Land of Eden*, i.e., North Carolina; and *A Progress to the Mines*.

D. Writers of political history

1. The South. Several historians, including Rev. WILLIAM STITH, author of *History of the First Discovery and Settlement of Virginia* (1747), a careful work based on original records of events to 1624.

2. The Middle Colonies
   a) WILLIAM SMITH, a Tory, ignorant of Dutch, author of *History of New York* (1757).
   b) SAMUEL SMITH, a Quaker, author of a dull but reliable *History of New Jersey* (1765).

3. New England
   a) Rev. THOMAS PRINCE (1687–1758). His *Chronological History of New England* (1736–55) brought the history of the Colonies down only to 1633; distinguished as the first history in English written with modern ideal of scientific accuracy.

III. Religious and Controversial Works

A. Religion and theology the chief concern of writers in the seventeenth century; in the eighteenth century the increase of political writings and of verse indicates a shift of interest. Controversy in the seventeenth century chiefly over church organization and government; in the eighteenth, over doctrine.

B. Aristocracy versus democracy in the churches, 1620–1720

1. Conflict between democratic Separatist tendencies, exemplified first at Plymouth, and the establishment of a Puritan presbyterian hierarchy in the church, favored by the educated and well-to-do clergy.

2. Conservative and aristocratic writers

 a) Immigrants

   (1) JOHN COTTON (1585–1652), first minister at Boston, placed
        church above state, and disbelieved in democracy in
        church and state; wrote *The Keys of the Kingdom of
        Heaven, and the Power Thereof* (1644), *The Way of the
        Congregational Churches Cleared*, etc.

   (2) THOMAS SHEPARD (1605–49), minister at Cambridge, was
        a pulpit orator of great sweetness and power.

   (3) NATHANIEL WARD (died in England, 1652) wrote *The
        Simple Cobbler of Aggawam* (1647), a brilliant attack on
        toleration and democracy, but best known for its satire on
        women, etc.

   (4) JOHN ELIOT,* in *The Christian Commonwealth* (London,
        1659), sketches an ideal state dominated by the church
        hierarchy.

 b) The native clergy

   (1) INCREASE MATHER (1639–1723), educated at Harvard and
        Dublin, pastor of Old North Church for sixty-four years,
        president of Harvard. Autocratic and masterful, leader
        in organizing ecclesiastical control; great preacher and
        pamphleteer. Works: *Important Truths about Conversion*
        (1674), *A Discourse concerning Baptism* (1675), *Cases of
        Conscience concerning Witchcraft* (1693), etc.

   (2) COTTON MATHER (1663–1728), grandson of John Cotton,
        son of Increase Mather and his assistant and successor at
        Old North Church. Continued his father's struggle for
        ecclesiastical domination but with decreasing success;
        best represents in his life and works the intensity and nar-
        rowness of American Puritanism. Indefatigable preacher
        and writer; published over 470 works—most important
        his *Magnalia Christi Americana, or The Ecclesiastical His-
        tory of New England* (1702), dealing in seven books with
        the founding of the Colonies, lives of governors and clergy,
        Harvard College and its graduates, the doctrine and dis-

cipline of the churches, Divine providences, and contro-
versies with heretical sects. Also wrote *Bonifacius or
Essays to Do Good* (1710), etc.

3. Liberal and democratic writers

    a) ROGER WILLIAMS (1606?–83), educated at Cambridge Uni-
versity, championed "a democratic church in a democratic
society." Attacked the tyranny of the leaders of the
church; driven from Massachusetts Bay and founded Provi-
dence, R.I. Works include: *The Bloudy Tenent of Persecution* (London, 1644), etc., a controversy with John Cotton on
toleration.

    b) THOMAS HOOKER (1586–1647), of Hartford, naturally auto-
cratic but leader of a schism in the church, wrote *Survey of the
Summe of Church Discipline*, which partly favors democracy
in the churches.

    c) JOHN WISE (1652–1725), of the Second Church of Ipswich,
published *The Churches Quarrel Espoused* (1713 ?) and *Vindica-
tion of the New England Churches* (1717) in reply to the pro-
posals of the conservatives for closer union of the churches.
Vigorous and independent.

4. Decline of clerical power after 1720. Struggle for ecclesiastical
democracy succeeded by a parallel political struggle.

C. Defense and modification of Calvinistic theology, 1720–89

  1. The Arminians attacked the doctrines of determinism (i.e.,
absence of individual freedom of choice between right and
wrong) and irresistible grace or predestination (i.e., man's
foreordination to be saved or lost). Rationalists, or deists,
belittled the evil in the plan of the world; cf. Pope's *Essay on
Man*. Enthusiasts (e.g., Whitefield, the evangelist, leader of
the "Great Awakening" of 1740) encroached on the powers and
privileges of the regular clergy; led to schism in the church.

  2. JONATHAN EDWARDS (1703–58)

    a) Graduated from Yale, 1720; minister at Northampton,
1727–50, where he began the Great Awakening; missionary
to the Indians, 1751; president of Princeton, 1758.

    b) Of subtle and powerful intellect, poetic sensitiveness, and
spiritual intensity; a logical yet eloquent preacher, famous

for his pictures of the pains of hell, as in his sermon, *Sinners in the Hands of an Angry God* (1741); style orderly, clear, simple, vivid.

   c) Most important work the treatise on the *Freedom of the Will* (1754), defending the Calvinistic determinism and predestination; gives him rank of greatest American philosophical writer.

3. CHARLES CHAUNCY (1705–87) and JONATHAN MAYHEW (1720–66) modify the sterner Calvinistic doctrines. Mayhew points the way to Unitarianism.

4. SAMUEL JOHNSON (1696–1772), a disciple of Bishop Berkeley, took a moderate theological position; wrote *Introduction to the Study of Philosophy* (1731) and *Elementa Philosophica* (1752).

5. JOHN WOOLMAN, the Quaker (1720–72). His *Journal* emphasizes "duties rather than doctrine," in a gracious spirit.

IV. Newspapers and Magazines

A. Begin in the Colonial period; varied and with some literary character; contain news, controversial articles, Addisonian essays; material often borrowed from English publications.

B. Some of the more important were
1. Newspapers: JAMES FRANKLIN's *New England Courant* (1721–26); BENJAMIN FRANKLIN's* *Pennsylvania Gazette* (1729–66); *South Carolina Gazette; Virginia Gazette; Boston Gazette* (1719–83); ISAIAH THOMAS'* *Massachusetts Spy* (1770–83).
2. Magazines: FRANKLIN's* *The General Magazine* (1741); GRIDLEY's *The American Magazine; The New England Magazine.*

V. Verse

A. Seventeenth-century verse
1. Its manner is imitative and mostly uninspired.
2. Descriptive, narrative, and expository works dealing with the new country:
   a) WILLIAM MORRELL: *Nova Anglia* (1625).
   b) BENJAMIN TOMPSON (1644–1714): *New England's Crisis* (*ca.* 1675), an epic on King Philip's War.

    c) PETER FOLGER (1617-90): *A Looking Glass for the Times* (1677), a plea for toleration.

    d) JOHN HOLME: *A True Relation of the Flourishing State of Pennsylvania* (1686).

3. *The Whole Booke of Psalmes* [*Bay Psalm Book*] (1640), a very poor metrical version of the Psalms.

4. Memorial poems. Fantastic, "conceited," unpoetical; follow English models, especially the poems of Quarles; mostly in pentameter couplets. Chiefly elegies by the clergy on the clergy.

    a) B.W. [BENJAMIN WOODBRIDGE?]: "Upon the Tomb of the Most Reverend John Cotton" (1669).

    b) URIAN OAKES: "An Elegie upon the Death of the Reverend Mr. Thomas Shepard" (1677).

    c) SAMUEL WIGGLESWORTH's "Funeral Song" (1709) in phrasing suggests Elizabethan and Miltonic influence.

5. ANNE BRADSTREET (1613-72). The first Colonial writer with signs of poetic endowment; largely influenced by Sylvester— translator of Du Bartas' *Divine Weeks* (1598)—Quarles, and other inferior English poets; somewhat by Spenser.

    a) "The Foure Monarchyes" (in *The Tenth Muse*, etc., 1650), a rhymed chronicle.

    b) "Contemplations" (1678) shows sweetness in nature description and an Elizabethan vein of meditation on the transitoriness of mortal things, with Puritan religious tone.

6. Rev. MICHAEL WIGGLESWORTH (1631-1705) versified the theology of Puritanism in "jigging rhymes."

    a) "The Day of Doom" (1662) presents with harsh concreteness the Calvinistic Day of Judgment; an extremely popular work.

    b) *God's Controversy with New England*, inspired by the drought of 1662.

    c) *Meat out of the Eater* (1669) deals with the "necessity and usefulness of afflictions."

7. REV. EDWARD TAYLOR (*ca.* 1644-1729), minister at Westfield, Mass., wrote "metaphysical" poems of great distinction, first published (in part) in 1937.

B. Eighteenth-century verse to 1765
1. Poetry still imitative, at first of Waller, but mainly of Pope, who was known by 1715; still small in amount.
2. Representative writers
   a) Rev. MATHER BYLES (1707–88): "To His Excellency Governor Belcher" (1732).
   b) JOSEPH GREEN (1706–80) was broadly humorous; wrote Hudibrastic verse.
   c) Rev. JOHN ADAMS (1704–40) was more natural than Pope and showed influence of Milton.
   d) EBENEZER COOK (?– ?): "The Sot-Weed Factor" (1708), a humorous narrative of life in Maryland.
   e) THOMAS GODFREY* (1736–63), of Philadelphia, showed great promise.
      (1) *Juvenile Poems* are imitative; some, however, healthily influenced by Chaucer.
      (2) *The Prince of Parthia* (written 1759), a tragedy, is crude but powerful.

THE PERIOD OF THE REVOLUTION
1765-1789

I. General Characteristics

A. Main interest of the country political; writing largely patriotic and controversial; religious questions subordinated; small inspiration to belles-lettres and few writers of a purely literary character.

B. Dominance of New England less pronounced, yet the parts of the country still isolated; rival literary centers in Hartford, New Haven, New York, and Philadelphia.

II. Miscellaneous Prose

A. BENJAMIN FRANKLIN* (1706-90)

1. A "Yankee," typical of the century; wider range of accomplishments than any other American of the period—printer and publisher, public servant, statesman, foreign ambassador, scientist, philosopher, author. Combines "hardness, shrewdness, ingenuity, practical sense, frugality, industry, self-reliance."

2. Essays—urbane, witty, fanciful

.a) *Dogood Papers* (1722) and *Busy-Body Papers* (1728-29), on the model of Addison.

b) The "bagatelles" (1778-80), including "The Whistle" and "Dialogue between Franklin and the Gout," show French influence.

3. *Poor Richard's Almanac* (1732-57; for the years 1733-58). The sayings of "Poor Richard," later collected and published separately as *The Way to Wealth* (1760, etc.), are homely and witty practical philosophy.

4. Scientific works include *Experiments and Observations in Electricity* (1751).

5. Political essays. All clear, vigorous; some equal Swift in satire: the report of his *Examination* (before the House of Commons) on American conditions (1766), *An Edict by the King of Prussia* (1773), *Rules by Which a Great Empire may be Reduced to a Small One* (1773), etc.

9

6. His *Autobiography* (written 1771, 1784–89), greatest of his works, sketches his life to 1759.

B. Political writings. Chiefly "state papers, speeches, and essays," though the letters and poetry of the time have a political side. The prose is marked by vigor, dignity, and intellectual force; had important influence upon later thought and style of American literature.

1. JAMES OTIS (1725–83). Orator, as in great speech against writs of assistance (1761). Essayist, as in the forceful and somewhat extravagant *Rights of the British Colonies Asserted and Proved* (1764).

2. PATRICK HENRY (1736–99). Author of memorable and influential speeches at turning-points in the struggle of the Colonies for independence; considered greatest orator of his age.

3. SAMUEL ADAMS (1722–1803). Long career as essayist and political organizer.

4. JOHN ADAMS (1735–1826). Cousin of Samuel Adams, of trained legal mind; wrote controversial pamphlets.

5. JOHN DICKINSON (1732–1808) wrote the admirably vigorous and fair *Letters of a Farmer in Pennsylvania* (1767–68).

6. THOMAS JEFFERSON (1743–1826), in the *Declaration of Independence* (1776), phrased with eloquence and boldness the ideal of democracy as it had taken shape in America and in France.

7. THOMAS PAINE* (1737–1809), an Englishman, most famous for his radical *Rights of Man* (London, 1791–92) and *Age of Reason* (Part I, 1793 [?]; Part II, 1795), belongs also to American literature for (a) *Common Sense* (1776), an opportune, racy argument for independence; and (b) a series of sixteen stirring papers, *The Crisis* (1776–83), issued at critical moments during the war.

8. ALEXANDER HAMILTON (1757–1804)
   a) Showed precocious learning and skill in replies (1775) to the "Westchester Farmer's" pamphlets.
   b) Planned, and wrote the greater part[1] of the essays in, *The Federalist* (1787–88), a defense of the new constitution, which from its breadth and soundness has become nearly as authoritative as the Constitution itself.

[1] His collaborators were JAMES MADISON and JOHN JAY.

9. Loyalist writers include: DANIEL LEONARD; MARTIN HOWARD, author of *A Letter from a Gentleman at Halifax to His Friend in Rhode Island;* SAMUEL SEABURY, author of the "Westchester Farmer" pamphlets; JOSEPH GALLOWAY; and MYLES COOPER.

C. Histories, narratives, and personal records

1. Governor THOMAS HUTCHINSON (1711–80), in *The History of the Province of Massachusetts Bay* (3 vols., 1764, 1767, 1828). deals with events to 1774 in a conservative but in the main fair-minded and trustworthy manner.

2. Narratives of captivity during the Revolution were written by ETHAN ALLEN, THOMAS ANDROS, HENRY LAURENS, etc.

3. Travels and other historical materials
   a) Captain JONATHAN CARVER's *Travels* (1778) gives an in part plagiarized account of a journey as far as the headwaters of the Mississippi.
   b) WILLIAM BARTRAM's *Travels* (1791) combines scientific observation of nature in the South with romantic sentimentalizing of unsophisticated man and nature.
   c) ST. JEAN DE CRÈVECOEUR ["J. Hector St. John" on his title-page] (1735–1813), in *Letters from an American Farmer* (1782), wrote charming though somewhat sentimental descriptive essays on American life.

D. Magazines and literary essays

1. Two chief magazines, *The Pennsylvania Magazine*, edited by THOMAS PAINE* during 1775–76, and ISAIAH THOMAS's* *The Royal American Magazine*.

2. Essays imitated and borrowed from English periodicals
   a) FRANCIS HOPKINSON's* *A Pretty Story* (1774) reflects Colonial resentment of tyranny in an entertaining allegory.
   b) JOSEPH DENNIE (1768–1812) wrote the Addisonian *Lay Preacher* (1795–96; Second Series, 1816).

III. Verse of the Revolutionary Period

A. Increasing in quantity, still closely following the eighteenth-century English vogue of "long, didactic, descriptive, and philosophic" poems; "their heroic couplet is that of Pope or Goldsmith; their

blank verse is that of Thomson or Young." Show beginning of
national spirit in patriotic poems and satire. Quality sometimes
approaches that of the English prototypes.

B. Ballads and songs of the Revolution. Numerous; spirited; among
the best are "Nathan Hale" (1776) and FRANCIS HOPKINSON's*
"Battle of the Kegs" (1778).

C. Minor poets: PHILLIS WHEATLEY, a negress (*Poems*, 1773); THOMAS
COOMBE ("Peasant of Auburn," imitating "The Deserted Village,"
1775); JOSEPH BROWN LADD (*Poems of Arouet*, 1786); PETER
MARKOE* (*Miscellaneous Poems*, 1787); JONATHAN ODELL, a Tory
satirist.

D. The Hartford wits

1. Literary center of country shifted from Massachusetts and
Pennsylvania to Hartford and New Haven, where there was less
political ferment. This is the first important literary group.
All conservative; poems mostly long; satires the best.

2. JOHN TRUMBULL (1750–1831), besides minor poems, wrote:
The Progress of Dullness (1772, 1773) in Hudibrastic couplets,
satirizing colleges, fops, and coquettes; *An Elegy on the Times*
(1774); and *M'Fingal* (1775–82), his chief work, a burlesque
epic modeled on *Hudibras*, satirizing the Tories with rough
vigor and humor. With BARLOW, HUMPHREYS, and HOPKINS
wrote *The Anarchiad* (1786–87), a lively mock-heroic, on Shay's
Rebellion and other contemporary events.

3. TIMOTHY DWIGHT (1752–1817). Grandson of Jonathan
Edwards; president of Yale; most representative, though not
most gifted, of the group. Chief works: *The Conquest of Canaan*
(1785), a mediocre biblical epic, in the style of Pope's *Homer;*
The Triumph of Infidelity (1788), a theological satire; *Greenfield
Hill* (1794), in different meters in imitation of various English
poets, a heavily didactic poem, containing pleasant descriptions
of American scenes.

4. JOEL BARLOW (1754–1812), author of *The Vision of Columbus*
(1787), a philosophical poem; expanded it into *The Columbiad*
(1807), a dull epic of the discovery and settlement of America.
The Hasty-Pudding (1793), a mock-heroic, is entertaining

5. Minor members of the group were: DAVID HUMPHREYS, author of *The Happiness of America* (1786), etc.; LEMUEL HOPKINS; THEODORE DWIGHT; RICHARD ALSOP, author of *The Charms of Fancy* (written by 1788; published 1856).

E. PHILIP FRENEAU (1752–1832)

1. Foremost poet of the century in bulk of work, range, and power —"the only American poet before Bryant who possessed . . . . imagination, insight, and felicity of style." Editions of his poems published in 1786, 1788, 1795, 1809, and 1815.
2. Satires: vigorous or violent; influenced by Churchill and others. "The British Prison Ship" (1781; written 1780) and "The Political Balance" (1786) are political; those on American life include "The Village Merchant" (1795), "The New England Sabbath-Day Chase" (1795), and "A Journey from Philadelphia to New York" (1787).
3. Narrative and descriptive poems: show influence of Milton, Goldsmith, and Gray, and contain some beautiful lines; "Pictures of Columbus" (1788; written 1774?), "The Beauties of Santa Cruz" (written 1776), and "The House of Night" (written 1776), a powerful though crude "romantic" poem, are representative.
4. Lyrics: dealing with the Indian, as "The Indian Burying Ground" (1788), "The Indian Student" (1788); dealing with nature, as "The Wild Honeysuckle" (1788), "To a Caty-Did" (1815); with the sea, as "On the Death of Captain Nicholas Biddle" (1779), and "On the Memorable Victory Obtained by . . . Paul Jones" (written 1781). The best of the lyrics written between 1775 and 1790; marked by simplicity, restraint, and beauty.

IV. Beginnings of the Drama

See below, page 24.

NATIONAL LITERATURE TO 1870

GENERAL CHARACTERISTICS

I. **Underlying Tendencies**

A. Literature still colored by local differences; e.g., the educated and still somewhat Puritan New England, cosmopolitan New York, the slave-holding and aristocratic South. The West beginning to influence subject-matter, but has no centers of its own before 1860.

B. Still a parallelism with European and English literature, reflection of English Romantic movement, German metaphysics, and the later turn to realism. But American literature after 1800 not directly imitative in the same sense as before; literature as a profession is pursued by a rapidly increasing number of writers, and with substantial success.

II. **Dominance of New York and Pennsylvania (1789–1830)**

A. Philadelphia was the chief residence of the first novelist, Charles Brockden Brown, and was the center of an active group of dramatists and poets.

B. The other important authors of the time, Bryant, Irving, and Cooper, lived in or near New York.

III. **The Renascence of New England**

A. The second third of the century saw the renascence of New England as the intellectual and literary center of the United States, after the temporary leadership of Philadelphia and New York. The period marked by

1. Two great movements in thought, the leaders in both mainly Massachusetts men, spiritual heirs of the Puritans.

   a) Religious and philosophical—Unitarianism and Transcendentalism.

   b) Political—the anti-slavery movement, the impetus to which was moral and humanitarian.

Mastery of the literary art, partly foreshadowed by Bryant, but attained by writers of wider range of intellectual interests and greater variety of artistic powers.

B. Boston and Cambridge the center of a group of men of letters, the most famous in our literature in their various fields, the only two figures of first importance outside this group being Poe and Whitman: Longfellow and Whittier, poets; Lowell, poet and critic; Emerson, poet and philosopher; Holmes, poet, essayist, and novelist; Hawthorne, novelist and story writer; Thoreau, essayist; Prescott, Motley, and Parkman, historians; Webster and Phillips, orators. Their juxtaposition and intimacy justify the description of Boston as the "Athens of America," and the period as the "Golden Age of American Literature."

PROSE FICTION TO 1870

I. Beginnings of the Novel

A. English novelists read somewhat in America before the Revolution, but native novel begins late; novels considered immoral and dangerous. First American novels justified as true and edifying stories.

B. The domesticity, morality, and sensibility of Samuel Richardson are the chief influence in: Mrs. ANN ELIZA BLEECKER's *The History of Maria Kittle* (in *New-York Magazine*, 1790–91; separately, 1802) and *The Story of Henry and Anne* (written by 1783; published 1793); Mrs. SARAH WENTWORTH MORTON's* *The Power of Sympathy* (1789); SUSANNA H. ROWSON's *Charlotte Temple* (1794), *Trials of the Human Heart* (1795), *Reuben and Rachel* (1798), etc.; and Mrs. HANNAH W. FOSTER's *The Coquette* (1797). TABITHA G. TENNEY's *Female Quixotism* (1808) treats the same matters satirically.

C. *Modern Chivalry* (1792–1805), by HUGH HENRY BRACKENRIDGE* (1748–1816), of Pennsylvania, an amusing satire on American life, follows Cervantes, Rabelais, Le Sage, and Swift. ROYALL TYLER* (1758–1826), in *The Algerine Captive* (1799), is influenced by Smollett.

II. Charles Brockden Brown (1771–1810)

A. The first professional man of letters in America; the first novelist to demand serious attention; forerunner of Poe and Hawthorne in handling the psychology of terror. Influenced by the theories of the English political and philosophical radical, William Godwin, and by Godwin's use of the material of terror in *Caleb Williams* (1794), a novel of the English "School of Terror"; himself in turn influencing Shelley.

B. Works include six novels, the first four of the "Gothic" type, with special interest in morbid psychology: *Wieland* (1798), "a study of inherited religious mania induced by ventriloquism"; *Ormond* (1799), a study of a powerful, violent, and supremely selfish villain, closely resembling Godwin's hero, Falkland; *Arthur Mervyn* (1799, 1800), containing vivid pictures of a yellow-fever epidemic, and also showing the influence of Godwin; *Edgar Huntly* (1799), "a study of sleep walking and madness," also noteworthy for its introduction of American scenes and its pioneer treatment, in fiction, of the American Indian; *Clara Howard* (1801), and *Jane Talbot* (1804). The last two, studies of moral problems, in Richardson's letter form.

C. Also wrote *Alcuin: a Dialogue on the Rights of Women* (1797), *Thessalonica, a Roman Tale* (apparently a late work), and miscellaneous pamphlets and verses; was editor of two magazines and an annual register.

D. Literary characteristics. Style crude but powerful; little range or subtlety in characterization, but sharp and impressive presentation of mental states; scenes of horror extraordinarily vivid.

III. James Fenimore Cooper (1789–1851)

A. Born Burlington, N.J., September 15, 1789; at Yale three years; seaman and midshipman, 1806–11; married 1811; in Europe, 1826–33; died at Cooperstown, N.Y.; sturdy, quarrelsome, energetic.

B. Without direct literary origins, created the American novel of adventure, and has been the widest read of American novelists in America and abroad. Wrote thirty-two novels dealing with: (1) the sea, (2) the American frontier, (3) aspects of American life in New England and the Middle States, (4) European scenes. The best, with one exception, belong to the first or second group. Novels marked by (1) power of invention, directed mainly toward thrilling action, chiefly of conflict or of flight and pursuit; (2) intimate

knowledge of sea and of forests and woodcraft; (3) power in presenting certain elementary characters, the frontiersman, the sailor, the
crafty Indian; (4) colorlessness and conventionality in the other
male and nearly all the female characters; (5) a vein of poetry
which gives a romantic atmosphere to his nature scenes; (6) lack of
humor; and (7) an uneven and rather diffuse style.

C. Chief works

1. Of the sea: *The Pilot* (1824), with its portrait of Long Tom
   Coffin and Paul Jones; *The Red Rover* (1828); *The Water-Witch*
   (1830).

2. "Leatherstocking" tales: *The Deerslayer* (1841), *The Last of the
   Mohicans* (1826), *The Pathfinder* (1840), *The Pioneers* (1823),
   and *The Prairie* (1827), as here rearranged present significant
   episodes in the life of a pioneer and, together, "the New World's
   epic of action in the conquest of a continent." *The Last of the
   Mohicans* is the most vivid, *The Deerslayer* and *The Prairie* are the
   most poetical. Natty Bumpo has been called "the most memorable character of American fiction."

3. Other novels: *The Spy* (1821), his second, and his first successful,
   novel; has a semi-historical setting in Revolutionary days, and
   a great character in Harvey Birch, the spy. *Satanstoe* (1845)
   portrays Colonial life in New York.

IV. Nathaniel Hawthorne* (1804–64)

A. Born in Salem, July 4, 1804; graduated at Bowdoin, 1825; lived in
   Salem, Concord, Lenox, etc.; intimately associated with the other
   members of the New England group, especially the transcendentalists; in United States customs service; consul at Liverpool,
   1853–57; in Italy and England, 1858–60; died at Plymouth, N.H.,
   May 18, 1864.

B. Influenced by, and akin to, the European writers of the Romantic
   movement—with their interest in the individual, in man's relation
   to nature, in the struggle against convention, in the mysterious and
   the supernatural—and the Americans, Charles Brockden Brown and
   Poe. Differs from Brown and Poe in using the supernatural as a
   means to the unfolding of a moral situation. In his chief romances
   applied a searching test to the transcendental doctrines set forth

by Emerson in such essays as "Self Reliance," "Compensation," and "Circles," studying the actual effect of independence of convention, and of sin, in real life.

C. Author of tales and novels, largely with a background of Colonial life in New England, which he presents with great fidelity; works chiefly concerned with problems of the human soul, the inner drama of life. Characterized by (1) imagination of delicacy but of great power, especially in dealing with the supernatural; (2) considerable narrative skill, though swiftness often checked by contemplative, speculative, or descriptive passages; (3) the creation of unusual but convincing and absorbing characters; (4) a subtle and pervasive symbolism, sometimes taking the form of allegory; (5) finished artistry of structure and style.

D. Tales[1]

  1. *Twice-Told Tales* (1st series, 1837, 2d series, 1842), *Mosses from an Old Manse* (1846), and *The Snow Image and Other Twice-Told Tales* (1851) show a kindly interest in humanity, humor and satire, and love of nature, besides his constant imaginative use of the supernatural.

  2. *Grandfather's Chair* (1841–42) and *Biographical Stories for Children* (1842) charmingly retell history, chiefly early American, for the young.

  3. *A Wonder Book* (1851) and *Tanglewood Tales* (1853) refashion classical myths for children, with equal skill.

E. Romances

  1. *Fanshawe* (1828), his first published work, is a fantastic and unsuccessful romance of college life.

  2. *The Scarlet Letter* (1850), his most powerful story, is "a study of the effects of sin upon the soul." Scene, Puritan Boston of the seventeenth century; outward action slight, symbolism pervasive.

  3. *The House of the Seven Gables* (1851), less powerful and less gloomy, is laid in New England of the nineteenth century, but casts back to the superstitions and wrongs of the far past. Again interest in sin and retribution; but contrast and relief

For relation to the short story, cf. below, pp. 21–22.

    secured by introducing some light realism and humor and a pleasant love story.

  4. *The Blithedale Romance* (1852) tells with indifferent success the story of a communistic group like that which the transcendentalists formed at Brook Farm.

  5 *The Marble Faun* (1860) displays against an Italian background another drama of sin and its inner consequences, with a power and beauty close to that of *The Scarlet Letter*.

  6. Posthumous romances (unfinished): *The Dolliver Romance* (1864, 1876), *Septimius Felton* (1872), and *Dr. Grimshawe's Secret* (1883), similar studies on the elixir of life. an ancestral curse, etc., apparently show loss of power.

F. Miscellaneous: *Our Old Home* (1863), an imperfect, biased account of England and its people; *American Note-Books* (1868), *English Note-Books* (1870), *French and Italian Note-Books* (1872), vivid jottings of his observations, etc.

V. Minor Novelists

In each section of the country an increasing number of novelists, most of them now forgotten or living in a single work.

A. New England

  1. JOHN NEAL* (1793–1876), inspired by Cooper, wrote novels of Byronic rant and melodrama, including *Keep Cool* (1817), *Logan* (1822), *Seventy-Six* (1823), *Brother Jonathan* (1825) and *The Down-Easters* (1833).

  2. CATHERINE M. SEDGWICK (1789–1867) wrote historical romances, later turning to realism; her best works are *Redwood* (1824), *Hope Leslie* (1827), and *The Linwoods* (1835).

  3. LYDIA M. CHILD (1802–80), an active abolitionist, based her novels, as *The Rebels* (1822), on American history.

  4. DANIEL PIERCE THOMPSON (1795–1868) wrote *The Green Mountain Boys* (1840), an extremely popular story of Vermont and Ethan Allen, in the manner of Cooper.

  5. WILLIAM WARE (1797–1852) wrote the historical romances *Zenobia* (1838) and *Aurelian* (1848).

  6. OLIVER WENDELL HOLMES* (1809–94) wrote three novels, *Elsie Venner* (1861) *The Guardian Angel* 1867), and *A Mortal*

Antipathy (1885), all concerned with the influence of heredity. Interesting rather for the faithful portrayal of the New England scene and for their ideas than as works of the imagination.

7 HARRIET BEECHER STOWE (1812–96) wrote *Uncle Tom's Cabin* (1851–52), the most famous book connected with the Civil War an ill-constructed and unfair but eloquent and dramatic representation of slavery in the South. Her later stories of New England life, as *Old-Town Folks* (1869), have fewer faults and fewer virtues.

8. RICHARD HENRY DANA, JR. (1815–82), author of the vivid, auto‧biographical *Two Years before the Mast* (1840).

B. The Middle States

1. JAMES KIRKE PAULDING* (1778–1860), friend of Irving and collaborator with him in *Salmagundi* (1807–8), wrote novels touched with comedy, as the *The Dutchman's Fireside* (1831).

2. ROBERT MONTGOMERY BIRD* (1806–54) wrote *Nick of the Woods* (1837), a "tale of border warfare in 1782."

3. HERMAN MELVILLE (1819–91), wrote partly autobiographical romances of the South Seas in moods alien to his time. *Typee* (1846) and *Omoo* (1847) are light and exotic. In *Moby-Dick* (1851), his masterpiece, somewhat influenced by Hawthorne, the subtle rhythm of style unites vivid narrative, mystical revery, moral symbolism, and social satire.

C. The South. In the novel, as in poetry, still less productive than the North, largely because of social conditions and ideals.

1. JOHN PENDLETON KENNEDY (1795–1870) wrote *Horseshoe Robinson* (1835), a story of the Revolution in the Carolinas, and *Rob of the Bowl* (1838), novels influenced by Cooper but more largely based on fact; author also of *Swallow Barn* (1832), in the style of *Bracebridge Hall*, and of the biography, *Memoirs of the Life of William Wirt* (1849).

2. NATHANIEL BEVERLEY TUCKER (1784–1851) wrote a notable Virginian novel, *The Partisan Leader* (1836).

3. WILLIAM GILMORE SIMMS* (1806–70), of South Carolina, ranks next to Cooper as a romancer. Besides much poetry, he wrote— after the Godwinian novel, *Martin Faber* (1833)—*Guy Rivers* (1834), *The Yemassee* (1835), and a group of novels of the Revolu-

tion, the best being *The Partisan* (1835), *The Kinsmen* (1841),
and *Katharine Walton* (1851). The novels have no characters
comparable to Cooper's, but resemble Cooper's in merits and
defects; they contain stirring action, but show haste and fondness for melodrama.

4. JOHN ESTEN COOKE (1830–86), in *The Virginia Comedians* (1854)
and other novels, presents vivid romantic glimpses of Southern
life, somewhat in the manner of Simms.

VI. The Tale and the Short Story

A. Prior to Irving the short fictitious narrative was not thought of as
a special literary form; like its English cousins, the tales of Mrs.
Inchbald and Maria Edgeworth, it was used as a vehicle for moral
or religious instruction.

B. WASHINGTON IRVING* (1783–1859)

1. Primarily an essayist of the Addisonian type, he passes over
from the essay to the sketch and the tale. He gives it literary
flavor, humor, and some characterization; does not advance
the short story as a type by technical improvement of conception,
construction, or climax.

2. Among the best of his tales, presenting humorous or pathetic
incidents or characters from American or European life, are:
"Rip Van Winkle" and "The Legend of Sleepy Hollow" (in
The Sketch Book, 1819–20); "The Stout Gentleman" and "Dolph
Heyliger" (in *Bracebridge Hall*, 1822); and "The Story of the
Young Italian" and "The Devil and Tom Walker" (in *Tales of a
Traveller*, 1824).

C. NATHANIEL HAWTHORNE* (1804–64)

1. The story makes a definite advance in the hands of a conscious
artist; he (1) conceives the story as a unit, always with a sustained atmosphere and often with a single situation; (2) gives
the story a meaning—usually connected with a moral problem—
and a climax; (3) presents character in detail. The form,
however, remains flexible, and often is undramatic, as much
essay as narrative. Individual flavor results from his delicate
and wayward fancy, his fondness for symbolism, and his concern
with the study of a troubled conscience.

2. Representative tales are:
   a) From *Twice-Told Tales* (1837, 1842): "The Minister's Black Veil," "The May-Pole of Merry Mount," "The Gentle Boy," "Mr. Higginbotham's Catastrophe," "A Rill from the Town Pump," "Dr. Heidegger's Experiment," "Lady Eleanor's Mantle," "The Ambitious Guest."
   b) From *Mosses from an Old Manse* (1846): "Young Goodman Brown," "Rappaccini's Daughter," "The Celestial Railroad," "Feathertop," "Drowne's Wooden Image."
   c) From *The Snow Image and Other Twice-Told Tales* (1851): "The Snow Image," "The Great Stone Face," "Ethan Brand."

D. EDGAR ALLAN POE* (1809-49)

1. Born in Boston, January 19, 1809; father an actor; mother, an actress of English birth, died 1811, and Poe adopted by John Allan of Richmond. At school in England, 1815-20; a few months at University of Virginia, 1826; in army, 1827-29; West Point, 1830-31. Rest of life spent in literary work, contributing to and editing magazines in Richmond, New York, Philadelphia. First published *Tamerlane and Other Poems*, 1827. Married, 1836, a cousin, Virginia Clemm, then thirteen years old, who died in 1847. Poe naturally impulsive and erratic; his weaknesses exaggerated and health impaired by intemperance. Died October 7, 1849. Wrote literary criticism, tales, poems.

2. Tales, in their subject-matter and general manner, show influence of C. B Brown, the German writer E. T. A. Hoffmann, and other writers of the "Gothic" school, as well as that of later English writers; Poe, in turn, exerted great influence in America, England and France; originated the detective story. The character of his tales is determined by the combination in him of "analytic intellect and . . . . poetic imagination."

3. His most important contribution a theory of the short story—a unique or single effect, rigorous exclusion of every word not contributing to it. In his tales exemplifies this unity—secured by singleness of theme, symmetry of structure, sustained harmony of tone through management of setting and style

4. Most of the tales published originally in periodicals, beginning with "Metzengerstein" (1832). Publications in book form include: *The Narrative of Arthur Gordon Pym* (1838). *Tales of the Grotesque and Arabesque* (1840), *Tales* (1845).

5. The most successful tales, classified by type, are:

   a) Tales of ratiocination: "The Gold-Bug," "The Murders in the Rue Morgue," "The Mystery of Marie Rogêt," "The Purloined Letter." Show his power of analysis and vividness

   b) Tales of pseudo-science: "The Adventure of One Hans Pfaal," "The Balloon Hoax," "A Descent into the Maelstrom," "The Facts in the Case of M. Valdemar." Combine intellectuality with imagination and effects of horror.

   c) Tales of adventure and horror: "MS. Found in a Bottle," "The Pit and the Pendulum," "The Cask of Amontillado."

   d) Tales of conscience: "William Wilson," "The Black Cat," "The Tell-Tale Heart." Present terror of conscience, with stress not on the moral aspect of sin but on the sinner's horror of mind.

   e) Romances of death: "The Assignation," "The Masque of the Red Death," "The Fall of the House of Usher," "Ligeia." Aspects of death presented with most striking imagination and splendor of style.

   f) Sketches of natural beauty: "The Island of the Fay," "The Domain of Arnheim," "Landor's Cottage."

6. Literary qualities

   a) Distinguished by (1) imaginative power; (2) analytical power; (3) grasp of structure; (4) power of creating atmosphere, especially of splendid gloom, solemnity, and horror; (5) felicitous but studied style, cold yet eloquent, sometimes close to De Quincey.

   b) Lacks grasp on character and sense of reality (stories originate not in observation of life but in theses suggested by his reading); narrow in range of interests; morbid, without Hawthorne's wholesomeness in treatment of similar materials; humor limited, like De Quincey's to the elaborate and extravagant or grotesque.

E. Transition and experiment, 1850–70

1. Increased demand for stories on the part of magazines; founding of *Atlantic Monthly* in 1857; recognition that fiction had been "far off from life," and a considerable endeavor on the part of writers to convey an impression of actuality. Not much attention as yet to the structural form of the short story.

2. Chief writers of this time are:

   a) ROSE TERRY COOKE (1827–92), who aimed at realism in her first story in the *Atlantic*, "Miss Lucinda" (1861); and in a long succession of stories in *Somebody's Neighbors* (1881), *The Sphinx's Children and Other People's* (1886), and *Huckleberries* (1891), depicted New England life with humor and sentiment, but diffusely.

   b) FITZ-JAMES O'BRIEN (1828–62), who in "The Diamond Lens" (1858), "What Was It?" (1859), and "The Wonder-smith" (1859) showed a kinship to Poe.

   c) EDWARD EVERETT HALE (1822–1909), author of the famous tales, "My Double and How He Undid Me" (1859), *The Man without a Country* (1863), and "The Brick Moon" (1869); secures effect of reality, but the narrative is leisurely and loose.

   d) HARRIET PRESCOTT SPOFFORD (1835–1921), author of the high-colored, romantic, poetic, and clever, but excessively self-conscious "The Amber Gods," and the clever, precocious detective story, "In a Cellar" (in *The Amber Gods and Other Stories*, 1863), who later in life published a volume of more finished romantic tales, *Old Madame and Other Tragedies* (1899), and turned to realism in "A Village Dressmaker" and "A Rural Telephone" (in *The Elder's People*, 1920).

THE DRAMA TO 1870

I. Beginnings, 1756–87

A. Delayed by the opposition of the authorities, the drama began late; interest quickened by (1) college dramatic exercises, as FRANCIS HOPKINSON's* revision of Thomson's *Masque of Alfred*, and (2) the presentation of plays by the company of professional actors under Lewis Hallam and David Douglass, which gave performances

in 1754 and later. Pre-revolutionary plays include: GODFREY'S*
Prince of Parthia (acted, Philadelphia, 1767), a tragedy in blank
verse, showing the influence of Shakspere and of the "heroic
play" of the Restoration, the first native play to be acted; Major
ROBERT ROGERS' [?] *Ponteach: or the Savages of America* (1766),
on the cruelty of the whites; and Colonel THOMAS FORREST's [?] *The
Disappointment: or the Force of Credulity* (1767).

B. During the Revolution few plays written, almost none acted; of
   slight literary value, chiefly interesting for their political significance,
   satirical pictures of the times.
   1. Mrs. MERCY OTIS WARREN* (1728–1814): *The Adulateur* (1773),
      on the Boston massacre; *The Group* (1775), against the Loyalists.
   2. JOHN LEACOCK's [?] *The Fall of British Tyranny* (1776).
   3. Anonymous plays: *The Blockheads* (1776), against the British
      in Boston; *The Battle of Brooklyn* (1776), against the Americans.
   4. Plays of some literary aim, but unsuited for the stage: HUGH
      HENRY BRACKENRIDGE's* *The Battle of Bunker's-Hill* (1776)
      and *The Death of General Montgomery* (1777), in stiff blank
      verse; PETER MARKOE's* [?] *The Patriot Chief* (1784), an
      extravagant drama of Lydia.

II. The Drama from 1787 to 1870

A. From 1787 to 1825 theater increasingly popular; plays now written
   primarily for the stage; at first largely imitated or adapted from
   foreign works; mostly of small literary value.
   1. ROYALL TYLER,* in *The Contrast* (acted 1787[1]), the first Ameri-
      can comedy produced by professionals, introduced the Yankee
      as a stage character. Also wrote *May Day in Town or New
      York in an Uproar* (1787), a comic opera, and *A Georgia Spec or
      Land in the Moon* (1797).
   2. WILLIAM DUNLAP (1766–1839), author of sixty-five plays, many
      adapted from Kotzebue and other foreign playwrights, was
      manager of the American Company during 1796–1805; a most
      influential figure. His first acted play was *The Father of an Only
      Child* (New York, 1789); *Leicester* (1794) was the second Ameri-
      can tragedy produced; *André* (1798) dealt with the Revolution.

[1] From this point on, unless otherwise indicated, the dates given in connection
with plays are of first acting.

3. JAMES N. BARKER (1784–1858), of Philadelphia, wrote a comedy, *Tears and Smiles* (1807); *The Indian Princess* (1808), "probably the first dramatic version of the Pocahontas story"; *Superstition* (1824), on the witchcraft delusion.

4. JOHN HOWARD PAYNE (1791–1852), of New York, like Dunlap under foreign influence, wrote sixty-four plays. Best are *Brutus* (London, 1818); *Charles II* (London, 1824). His opera, *Clari* (1823), contains the song, "Home, Sweet Home."

B. Between 1825 and 1860 the theatrical center shifts from Philadelphia to New York; in 1825 first attempt to establish Italian opera; beginning of Edwin Forrest's career as actor. Period more significant and creative. Plays include tragedies, American historical dramas, comedies of contemporary manners, local plays, comedies of social satire, romantic comedy, melodrama, farce, and dramatized novels. Tragedies have most literary value.

1. Philadelphia dramatists

a) ROBERT MONTGOMERY BIRD* (1806–54), the novelist, wrote three tragedies, *The Gladiator* (1831), *Oralloosa* (1832), a Peruvian drama, and *The Broker of Bogota* (1834), a good example of romantic verse tragedy.

b) RICHARD PENN SMITH (1779–1854), author of *The Eighth of January* (1829), *The Deformed* (1830), *The Triumph at Plattsburg* (1830), etc.

c) ROBERT T. CONRAD (1810–58), author of *Jack Cade* (1835; rewritten as *Aylmere*, 1841), a vigorous but melodramatic play.

d) GEORGE HENRY BOKER (1823–90) wrote romantic tragedies distinguished for grasp of character and plot, and eloquent poetic style. The greatest, *Francesca da Rimini* (1855), was successfully revived as late as 1901. Others: *Calaynos* (London, 1849); *Leonor de Guzman* (1853); *The Betrothal* (1850), a comedy.

2. Other dramatists of some literary power, and their chief plays:

a) EPES SARGENT: *Velasco* (1837), a tragedy.

b) NATHANIEL PARKER WILLIS* (1806–67): *Bianca Visconti* (1837), a verse tragedy; *Tortesa, the Usurer* (1839), a romantic comedy in verse.

    c) CHARLOTTE BARNES CONNER: *Octavia Brigaldi* (1837); *The Forest Princess* (1848), one of a number of plays dealing with the story of Pocahontas.

    d) [1]ANNA OGDEN MOWATT* (1819–70): *Fashion* (1845), a skilful comedy of social satire; *Armand or The Child of the People* (1847), a blank verse comedy.

    e) GEORGE H. MILES: *Mohammed* (1851), a romantic tragedy.

3. Dramatized fiction. Many novels and stories dramatized; the two which have survived are: *Uncle Tom's Cabin*, in the version of G. L. AIKEN (1852); *Rip Van Winkle*, the present form by DION BOUCICAULT and JOSEPH JEFFERSON being the fourth dramatic reworking of Irving's tale.

POETRY, 1789–1830

I. Minor Poets before Bryant

A. Time of transition, as in England; old and new influences side by side in imitations of (1) Pope, Akenside, Collins, Goldsmith, and (2) Wordsworth, Southey, Byron, Scott, "Ossian." Lyric on a surer footing beside satiric and didactic poetry.

B. The older influence chiefly felt in

    1. Didactic poems; as

        a) ROBERT TREAT PAINE's *The Ruling Passion,* the Harvard Phi Beta Kappa poem of 1797, a happy imitation of Pope.

        b) JOSEPH STORY's *The Power of Solitude* (1804).

    2. Poems of wit and satire, including political satire; as

        a) Social satires, including PETER MARKOE's* *The Times* (1788), WINTHROP SARGENT's *Boston* (1803), and the anonymous *Breechiad* (1807).

        b) Political satires continuing the vein of the "Hartford Wits": WILLIAM CLIFFTON's* *The Group* (1795) and *Rhapsody on the Times* (1800); ALSOP,* HOPKINS,* and DWIGHT's* *The Political Green-House* (1799); MATHEW CAREY's attack on William Cobbett, *The Porcupiniad* (1799); and the anonymous *Democratiad* (1795) and *Guillotina* (1796), Federalist attacks on the Democrats; and *Aristocracy* (1795), a counterblast.

[1] Mrs. Mowatt by a second marriage became Mrs. Ritchie.

    c) THOMAS G. FESSENDEN (1771–1837) wrote *A Terrible Tractoration* (1803), a Hudibrastic satire on scientific inventions, and *Democracy Unveiled*, a virulent attack on Jefferson.

C. In the shorter poems the influence of various currents of Romanticism begins to appear, along with that of the predecessors of Romanticism, Collins, Gray, and Goldsmith.

    1. The Gothic tale and the romantic ballad

        a) WILLIAM MOORE SMITH's "The Wizard of the Rock" (1786), SARAH WENTWORTH MORTON's* "Ouâbi, an Indian Tale" (1790), JOHN B. LINN's "Valerian" (1805), a tale of shipwreck, and the ballads in JOSEPH HUTTON's *Leisure Hours* (1812) deal with the strange or the exotic.

        b) LUCIUS M. SARGENT's "Hubert and Ellen" (1812) and HENRY C. KNIGHT's* "Margaret Dwy" (in *The Broken Harp*, 1815) are Wordsworthian tales of humble life.

    2. Poems of nature show distinct increase in the appreciation of natural beauties, and greater simplicity and delicacy of style.

        a) There are meritorious lyrics by WILLIAM CLIFFTON,* ALEXANDER WILSON (also author of *The Foresters* [1809], a descriptive narrative), and HENRY C. KNIGHT (in *Poems*, 1821).

        b) WASHINGTON ALLSTON's "The Sylphs of the Seasons" (1813) is particularly graceful and fanciful.

        c) JOHN NEAL's* *The Battle of Niagara* (1818) has passages of eloquent romantic description.

    3. Other aspects of Romanticism

        a) Personal passion and Byronic or Keatsian melancholy scarcely appear.

        b) Sentiments of political revolt and aspiration for liberty absent because liberty supposedly attained; there are patriotic poems instead, such as

            (1) JOSEPH HUTTON's "The Field of Orleans" (1816) and NEAL's* *The Battle of Niagara*.

            (2) The songs, "Hail Columbia" (sung in 1798), and FRANCIS SCOTT KEY's "The Star-Spangled Banner" (1814).

II. William Cullen Bryant (1794–1878)

    A. Bred in western Massachusetts, where he spent his early manhood to 1825 in the practice of law, but for most of his life resident in

New York; for half a century editor of the *New York Evening Post;* critic, essayist, and first important American poet.

B. Important dates of publication include: "The Embargo" (1808), a precocious but unimportant satire on Jefferson's peace policy; "Thanatopsis" (written 1811; published, with "Inscription for the Entrance to a Wood," in *North American Review* for September, 1817), which brought him instant recognition as a poet; *Poems,* 1821; *Poems,* 1832, containing eighty-two new poems; seven latei volumes of poems, new and old, 1834–63. Also volumes of tales, letters, and addresses, and translations of the *Iliad* (1870) and the *Odyssey* (1871–72).

C. The poems are (1) purely meditative and moralizing, of the type of "The Ages," or (2) descriptive of aspects or phenomena of nature, as "A Winter Piece," "Summer Wind," etc., or, most often, (3) a combination of nature description and meditation or moralizing, as "Thanatopsis," "To a Waterfowl," and "The Evening Wind." The meditative poems chiefly in blank verse; the descriptive nature poems in blank verse or simple stanzaic forms. Besides sheer delight in nature, the poems present only a few elemental thoughts: (1) man as a part of the cosmic process, (2) life and death, (3) the purifying and elevating influence of nature on man, often in the form of a "broad survey" of man's activities against the background of the natural world. Religious and philosophical views orthodox and untranscendental.

D. Literary relations. Shows the influence of Blair, Kirk White, and others of the "Graveyard School" in "Thanatopsis"; in the meditative and nature poems in blank verse combines the influence of these and other eighteenth-century poets, as Thomson and Cowper, with that of Wordsworth and Southey; in subjects and manner of the simpler nature lyrics, as "The Yellow Violet," "Oh, Fairest of the Rural Maids," "To the Fringed Gentian," shows contact with Wordsworth's *Lyrical Ballads.*

E. General estimate

　　1. Lacks color, warmth, passion, and gift of metaphor; few memorable poetic phrases; not much range or flexibility.

　　2. Has imaginative eloquence, in a restricted field, which passes over sometimes into the declamatory and heavily didactic.

3. Deserves high rank for dignity, earnestness, and poise; intimate knowledge of nature; simplicity, clarity, and justness of phrase.

III. Contemporaries of Bryant to 1830

A. The minor poets combine provincialism of thought with small imaginative endowment and a tendency to echo the notes of the English Romanticists, especially Scott, Moore, Byron, Shelley. Often remembered for a single poem, they include

1. New York group

   a) JAMES KIRKE PAULDING,* influenced by Scott, author of *The Lay of the Scotch Fiddle* (1813), *The Backwoodsman* (1818).

   b) JOSEPH RODMAN DRAKE (1795–1820), best of his group, author of the charming fairy poem, *The Culprit Fay* (1819).

   c) FITZ-GREENE HALLECK (1790–1867), influenced by Byron, Campbell, Scott, who wrote vigorous tales and lyrics, "Fanny" (1819), "Marco Bozzaris" (1825), "Alnwick Castle" (1827), "Burns" (1827), etc.

   d) SAMUEL WOODWORTH (1785–1842), author of "The Old Oaken Bucket" (1826).

   e) GEORGE P. MORRIS (1802–64), author of "Woodman, Spare That Tree" (written 1837).

2. New England group

   a) RICHARD HENRY DANA (1787–1879), author of *The Buccaneer* (1827), a sea romance.

   b) Mrs. MARIA GOWEN BROOKS (1795–1845), influenced by Moore and Southey, wrote poems of sensuous atmosphere including *Judith, Esther, and Other Poems* (1820), and *Zóphiel, or The Bride of Seven* (1833).

   c) Mrs. LYDIA HUNTLEY SIGOURNEY (1791–1865), of Hartford Conn., extraordinarily popular for her commonplace sentimental and moralizing works.

   d) JAMES GATES PERCIVAL (1795–1856), influenced by Byron and Shelley, had poetic feeling but lacked finish and form; of his poems may be mentioned *Prometheus* (1820). "Seneca Lake" (1843), and three volumes of lyrical and meditative verse published under the caption *Clio* (1822–27).

3. Southern poets:

    a) RICHARD H. WILDE (1789–1847), author of the song, "My Life is Like the Summer Rose," and the Byronic *Hesperia* (1867).

    b) EDWARD COATE PINCKNEY (1802–28) wrote "graceful lyrics in the manner of Moore."

THE NEW ENGLAND POETS
1830–1870

I. Henry Wadsworth Longfellow (1807–82)

A. Born in Portland, Maine, February 27, 1807; classmate of Hawthorne at Bowdoin; traveled much abroad; professor of modern languages, at Bowdoin and Harvard, 1829–54; resident in Cambridge for forty-six years; LL.D., Cambridge University, D.C.L., Oxford; died March 24, 1882. Reflects the dominant mood of New England culture; the most popular and widely read American poet; translated into many languages.

B. Through visits abroad, in contact with European literature and culture, especially of Germany and Scandinavia. Echoes in his own works; many poems translated by him, especially from the German. Among American influences on him are those of Bryant and Irving.

C. Chief works

    1. Prose

        a) Lectures and critical essays, of small importance.

        b) Romances: *Outre-Mer* (1833–34), sketches of European travel; *Hyperion* (1839), an autobiographical romance full of German sentiment; *Kavanagh* (1849), a colorless novel of New England life. All reflect the influence of Irving's *Sketch Book;* of little permanent value.

    2. Poems. Published volumes include: *Voices of the Night* (*1839*) *Ballads and Other Poems* (1841), *Poems on Slavery* (1842), *The Belfry of Bruges and Other Poems* (1845), etc.; last volume, *In the Harbor* (1882).

        a) Lyrics and other short poems:

            (1) Didactic pieces: "The Psalm of Life," etc.

(2) Narrative-descriptive sketches of homely life and the affections: "The Village Blacksmith," "The Old Clock on the Stairs," "The Children's Hour," etc.

(3) Ballads: "The Wreck of the Schooner Hesperus," "The Skeleton in Armor," etc.

(4) Nature poems and poems of the sea: "Rain in Summer," "Hymn to the Night," "The Secret of the Sea," "My Lost Youth," etc.

(5) Poems of slavery.

(6) Sonnets.

b) Narrative poems

(1) *Evangeline* (1847), sweet, sentimental, pathetic tale of lovers separated at the time of the expulsion of the Acadians; in hexameters of uneven quality, but often plaintively musical; possibly his greatest poem.

(2) *The Song of Hiawatha* (1855) tells Indian legends, mainly from Schoolcraft, in a rapid trochaic meter modeled on that of the Finnish epic, *Kalevala*; form admirably suited to the simple, naïve materials.

(3) *The Courtship of Miles Standish* (1858), in hexameters, gives "a sympathetic and truthful picture of the early days of Plymouth Colony"; has humor, characterization, and more strength than *Evangeline*.

(4) *Tales of a Wayside Inn* (3 series, 1863–74), mostly short tales retold, with a connecting thread of narrative; graceful but not striking, except for "Paul Revere's Ride" and "The Saga of King Olaf."

c) Dramatic poems. On the whole, his least successful work; the best are *The Golden Legend* (1851) and *Michael Angelo* (1883). Others are *The Spanish Student* (1843), *The New England Tragedies* (1868), *The Divine Tragedy* (1871), *Judas Maccabæus* (1872), and *The Masque of Pandora* (1875).

d) Translations

(1) Graceful renderings of German and other lyrics and ballads, in large numbers.

(2) *The Divine Comedy of Dante Aligheri* (1867–70), painstakingly literal, elegant, and dignified, but stiff.

D. General estimate
   1. Distinction (*a*) as a graceful and moving story-teller in verse, (*b*) as a transmitter of European culture and romance to America, (*c*) for the fineness of temper and character which colors all his works and was largely responsible for his great popularity, (*d*) for the simplicity, musical quality, and variety of his versification.
   2. Fails of greatest eminence because of lack of pronounced originality, passion, and intellectual vigor.

II. John Greenleaf Whittier (1807–92)
   A. Born in Haverhill, Mass., December 17, 1807; reared and lived in rural New England; educated in district school and Haverhill Academy; taught school; as a young man active in politics; fought long against slavery; edited various journals; after 1840 lived at Amesbury; died September 7, 1892. A Quaker.
   B. Literary influences in youth, the Bible, Burns, Scott; later a wide reader.
   C. Poems
      1. First poem published in 1826; first volume, *Legends of New England* (1831); many other volumes, the last, *At Sundown* (1892; privately printed, 1890). His poetry does not show distinct periods of growth or, except for slavery, definite changes in fields of interest.
      2. Poems dealing with slavery (in various volumes, 1837 and later). The largest group of his poems; more fiery than the anti-slavery poems of the other New England poets; splendidly indignant and often effectively rhetorical, but mostly of slight poetic value. Most successful are: "Massachusetts to Virginia" (1843); "Ichabod" (1850), on Webster's supposed apostasy in regard to slavery; "The Slave-Ships" (1834); "Randolph of Roanoke" (1847); "The Kansas Emigrants" (1854); and "Brown of Ossawatomie" (1859).
      3. Ballads and other narrative poems. The ballads considered the best in American literature: themes historical, legendary, or purely imaginative; style simple, flowing, picturesque, often vigorous and racy, sometimes diffuse; faithful to atmosphere of time and place; often with a moralizing conclusion. Among the best are:

a) Ballads: "The Witch's Daughter,"[1] "Skipper Ireson's Ride," "How the Women Went from Dover," "The Garrison of Cape Ann," "The Sisters," "Barbara Frietchie," "Amy Wentworth," "Maud Muller."

b) Short narratives with personal coloring: "My Playmate," "Telling the Bees," "The Barefoot Boy," and "In School-Days"; these have simplicity, tenderness, and are valuable as a record of New England country life akin to that of *Snow-Bound*.

c) *Snow-Bound* (1866), a narrative-descriptive idyl, commonly regarded as Whittier's greatest work, gives an intimate picture of a typical New England family shut in on its farm by a winter's storm; valuable as a "social document," vivid in its portraits, it shows Whittier's sweetness, tender humor, moral elevation, and homely idiomatic style.

4. Occasional and personal poems are numerous; marked by sincerity of feeling, often not highly poetical or distinguished by wit, yet occasionally very happy, as, "Centennial Hymn" (1876), "Garrison" (1879), and his tributes to Longfellow and Holmes.

5. Religious poems. A religious note in a large part of his work; elevated and intense but not dogmatic. See especially, "The Eternal Goodness" (1865), "Our Master" (1866), and the poems of religious questioning, such as "My Soul and I," "Questions of Life," and "The Shadow and the Light."

D. Prose. Considerable in amount, largely controversial and of no literary significance. *Margaret Smith's Journal* (1849), a fictitious record of Colonial days, is faithful to the spirit of the times.

E. General estimate

1. Kept from very high rank by limited horizon, diffuseness, and defects of meter and rhyme.

2. Master of simple, sincere, racy style, with sometimes extremely happy phrasing.

3. Distinguished by nobility of character, strong moral and religious feeling; a homely, unbookish poet, full of the spirit of old New England.

---

[1] Enlarged and republished as *Mabel Martin*.

III. James Russell Lowell* (1819–91)
   A. Born in Cambridge, Mass., February 22, 1819; educated at Harvard
      practiced law; professor at Harvard, in succession to Longfellow
      1856–77; editor of *Atlantic Monthly* and *North American Review*.
      Minister to Spain, 1877–80; Minister to England, 1880–85; D.C.L.
      Oxford; died August 12, 1891.
   B. Poems
      1. Early poems. Show influence of English Romanticists, Words-
         worth, Coleridge, Shelley, Keats, and of Tennyson; but possess
         an original quality in tone and in adaptation to native materials.
         Characteristic are: "The Sirens" (1840), "To Perdita Singing"
         (1841), "Rhœcus" (1843), "A Legend of Brittany" (1843).
      2. Nature poems. Often of a high quality; vivid and rich in
         poetic coloring, with strong emotion and moral dignity, as,
         "An Indian-Summer Reverie" (1847), "To the Dandelion"
         (1845), "Under the Willows" (1868), and the descriptive pre-
         ludes in *The Vision of Sir Launfal* (1848).
      3. Serio-comic poems show maturer powers
         a) *A Fable for Critics* (1848) hits off contemporary writers with
            wit, penetration, and good nature.
         b) *The Biglow Papers* (1st series, 1848; 2d series, 1867, collected
            from magazines) comments, in the Yankee dialect, with racy
            humor, on slavery, war, and the politics of the Mexican and
            the Civil wars.
      4. Odes and memorial poems, marked by nobility, dignity, and
         eloquence, though not perfectly sustained in manner or concep-
         tion.
         a) *Ode Recited at the Harvard Commemoration* (1865) presents a
            famous sketch of Lincoln.
         b) *Under the Old Elms* (1875) sketches the portrait of Washington.
         c) Others celebrate the anniversary of the fight at Concord
            Bridge and the Declaration of Independence.
      5. Personal poems, graceful, sometimes sentimental, sometimes
         philosophical; written at intervals throughout his life.
         a) The earlier are more lyrical and sentimental; as, "The
            Changeling" (1847), "The First Snow-Fall" (1849), "Auf
            Wiedersehn" (1854), etc.

      b) The later are more intellectual, as, *The Cathedral* (1869) and "Agassiz" (1874), in both of which he touches on the modern problem of reconstructing religious belief.

C. Prose essays. Cf. below, page 53.

D. General estimate

    1. The foremost American man of letters, in the special sense, by virtue of his versatility as "poet, essayist, humorist, editor, teacher, scholar . . . . diplomat . . . . letter writer"; prose and poetry alike in range of interest, cultivation, poise, humor, and strength.

    2. The poetry suffers from unevenness of poetic conception and style, and lack of singleness and compression.

IV. Oliver Wendell Holmes* (1809–94)

A. Born in Cambridge, August 29, 1809, of old New England stock; graduated at Harvard, 1829; studied law, and then medicine, in Boston and Paris; physician, Boston, 1836–39; Professor of Anatomy, Dartmouth, 1839–40, Harvard, 1847–82; Litt.D., Cambridge; LL.D., Edinburgh; D.C.L., Oxford; died October 7, 1894.

B. Successful lecturer, sound scientist, early noted locally as poet and wit, he attained literary fame late, with the publication of the *Autocrat* papers in the *Atlantic Monthly* (1857–58). Thoroughly of America and New England, he was aristocratic of temper and conservative in his literary ideals and political views, but through his scientific studies a vigorous radical in theology. Author of three novels, an important body of miscellaneous prose, and several volumes of poems (1836–92).

C. Poems

    1. Serious lyrical poems: "Old Ironsides" (1830), which first brought him fame; "The Chambered Nautilus" (1858), often considered his greatest poem; "Under the Violets" (1859), illustrative of his sentiment; and the two great hymns (1859), "Hymn of Trust" and "A Sun-Day Hymn."

    2. Serio-comic and comic lyrical poems. More numerous and more characteristic; best examples in America of "familiar verse." Some purely humorous, as, "The Height of the Ridicu-

lous" (1830), "My Aunt" (1831), "The Comet" (1832), and "Daily Trials" (1833). The majority blend humor with a touch of pathos or sentiment, or adroitly set forth an idea, as, "The Last Leaf" (1831), one of his happiest successes; "To an Insect" (1831), on the katydid; "On Lending a Punch-Bowl" (1849); "Latter-Day Warnings" (1857), which laughs at the Adventists; "Contentment (1858); and "Dorothy Q" (1871), graceful and tender guessing at an ancestress' story.

3. Narrative poems. Mostly brief, sometimes close to the lyrical; same variation of tone: "The Ballad of the Oyster-Man" (1830); "The Stethoscope Song" (1848); "The Deacon's Masterpiece, or the Wonderful One-Hoss Shay" (1858), a witty and spirited story with a veiled attack on the "logic" of Calvinistic theology; its offshoot, "How the Old Horse Won the Bet" (1876), and its "mathematical" cognate, "Parson Turell's Legacy" (1858); the stirring "Grandmother's Story of Bunker-Hill Battle" (1875); and "The Broomstick Train" (1890), which connects Colonial witches and electric cars.

4. "Occasional" poems. A large number, aptly combining wit with sentiment suited to the occasion.

   a) Poems of the Class of '29: "The Boys" (1859), "The Old Man Dreams" (1861), "Bill and Joe" (1868), "After the Curfew" (1890), etc.

   b) On persons, including Webster (written 1855–56), Burns (written 1856), Lowell, Longfellow, and Whittier.

   c) More didactic pieces, such as "Poetry: A Metrical Essay" (1836) and "Urania: A Rhymed Lesson" (1846).

D. General estimate of the poems

   1. Points of view of the scientist and the man of letters, of the Bostonian and the cosmopolitan, of the critic and the lover of his fellows, happily mingled.

   2. Distinguished, like the eighteenth-century poetry which he admired, by flashing wit, penetrating but kindly satire, grace and finish of metrical form and phrasing.

   3. Intellect and fancy predominate over the imagination. Except in a few pieces, therefore, his poetry is not of the first rank.

V. Ralph Waldo Emerson* (1803–82)

A. Born in Boston, May 25, 1803; graduated at Harvard, 1821; teaching, 1821–26; Harvard Divinity School, 1825–28; pastor, Old North Church, Boston, 1829–32; in Europe, 1832–33, 1847–48, 1872–73; residence in Concord, 1834–82; lecturer, 1832–72; died April 27, 1882.

B. Though chiefly famous for his philosophical writings in prose, Emerson wrote much poetry of essentially the same character, with respect to subjects and merits, as his essays.

1. Personal and nature poems. Have more feeling, less coldness, than his other poems.

   a) Nature poems, full of striking images, showing unusual powers of observation and phrasing; as, "The Rhodora" (written 1834), "The Humble-Bee" (written 1837), "My Garden" (written 1846), "Seashore" (written 1857). Also many descriptive passages in other poems.

   b) Poems of personal feeling: "Good-Bye" (written 1823), "Written in Naples" (written 1833), reflecting his grief over the death of his first wife; "Threnody" (written 1842–46), on the death of his son, Waldo; "Terminus" (written 1866), on the end of life.

   c) Tributes to friends, as "Webster" (written 1834), and "Woodnotes I" (1840), describing Thoreau.

2. "Occasional" and patriotic poems, among them the "Concord Hymn" (1837), one of his most flawless pieces.

3. Philosophical poems

   a) Sometimes personal in form with simple, concrete imagery, as "Holidays" (1842), "Forbearance" (1842), "The Apology" (1847), justifying his meditative seclusion, and "Days" (1851).

   b) Often abstract, though vivid; frequently difficult to interpret without knowledge of the essays, as, "Each and All" (written 1834), on the interdependence of all forms of beauty; "The Problem" (written 1839); "Compensation" (1841); "The Sphinx" (1841), which phrases Emerson's central doctrine of "The One in Many"; "The World-Soul" (1847); and "Brahma" (1857).

C. General estimate of the poems
   1. Merit of moral elevation, individuality, insight, and brilliant poetic phrase.
   2. Metrically unskilful, unity frequently ill-sustained, thought often cryptic, general effect eccentric.

VI. Minor New England Poets

A. WILLIAM WETMORE STORY (1819–95), a Massachusetts lawyer, lived in Italy after 1848, where he became a famous sculptor. Wrote excellent verse and prose, including graceful Tennysonian lyrics, and dramatic monologues in the manner of Browning, such as "The Confessional" (written 1855), an intense tale of jealous murder, and "A Roman Lawyer in Jerusalem" (1870), an adroit defense of Judas Iscariot.

B. THOMAS WILLIAM PARSONS (1819–92), a Boston dentist, translator of Dante's *Inferno* (1843–67), had an exquisite gift in a narrow field; best known for his "On a Bust of Dante" (1854).

C. Others are: SAMUEL F. SMITH (1808–95), author of "America" (1832); SARAH H. WHITMAN (1803–78), Poe's friend; ALBERT PIKE (1809–91), author of *Hymns to the Gods* (1829–45); SAMUEL LONGFELLOW (1819–92), brother of the poet, who wrote many hymns; JULIA WARD HOWE (1819–1910), author of "Battle Hymn of the Republic" (1862); JOSIAH G. HOLLAND (1819–81), lecturer and editor, who wrote popular but commonplace poems, including the versified novels *Bitter-Sweet* (1859) and *Kathrina* (1867).

POETS OUTSIDE NEW ENGLAND
1830–1870

1. Edgar Allan Poe* (1809–49)

A. Poe's theory of poetry well defines his own practice: (1) poetry is "the rhythmical creation of beauty"; (2) a poem has "for its immediate object, pleasure, not truth"; (3) passion and humor out of place; (4) sadness the best "tone"; (5) the lyric the only true poem, a long poem being a "contradiction in terms."

B. Early poems, in his first two volumes, *Tamerlane and Other Poems* (1827), and *Al Aaraaf, Tamerlane, and Minor Poems* (1829).

1. Obviously, prentice work; his only long poems; hazy in structure and idea, imitative in style. "Tamerlane," a slight Byronic tale; "Al Aaraaf" has Shelleyan sensuousness. The influence of Coleridge also appears here and later.
2. Suggestion of haunting beauty already present; occasional magic phrases.

C. Poems of his maturity
1. Two volumes of collected poems published during his life, *Poems* (1831), and *The Raven and Other Poems* (1845). Poems mostly first published separately in magazines; final form showed extensive happy revisions.
2. Subjects
   a) Death, especially "the death of a beautiful woman," as in "The Sleeper" (1831), "Lenore" (1831), "The Conqueror Worm" (1843), "The Raven" (1845), and the partly autobiographical "Ulalume" (1847) and "Annabel Lee" (1849).
   b) Fantasy and the world of spirits, as in "Israfel" (1831), "The City in the Sea" (1831), and "The Haunted Palace" (1839), which describes madness with gruesome symbolism.
   c) Personal poems, as the flawless "To Helen" (1831); the later "To Helen" (1848), on Mrs. Whitman, the poetess; and the sonnet to Mrs. Clemm, "To My Mother" (1849).
   d) Metrical exercises, as "The Bells" (1849).
3. Form and mood. These interested Poe more than ideas. Striking characteristics are:
   a) Haunting melody, highly original in effect, though akin to that of Coleridge.
   b) Poetic phrase rich in color and power of suggestion.
   c) Striking unity of emotional tone, through suggestions of beauty, gloom, or horror, and the use of the mystical or symbolic.
   d) A happy symmetry of structure in some poems.
4. Defects
   a) Narrowness of his range, indicated by virtual absence of poems dealing with normal human observations and experience, nature, love of the living, adventure, human characters, meditations or observations about life.

b) Lack of moral interest; unwholesomeness of spirit.

c) Impression of artificiality.

II. Minor Southern Poets

A. WILLIAM GILMORE SIMMS* (1806–70), of South Carolina, novelist, biographer, poet, published a dozen volumes of poems.

  1. The early volumes, which show the influence of Wordsworth, Byron, and Moore, are weak.

  2. Later wrote a considerable number of spirited narrative and dramatic poems, including *Atalantis; a Story of the Sea* (1832), influenced by *Comus*, which contains graceful songs, *The Cassique of Accabee* (1849), and many of the pieces in *Poems* (1853).

B. PHILIP PENDLETON COOKE (1816–50), of Virginia, brother of John Esten Cooke, published one volume, *Froissart Ballads and Other Poems* (1847), containing bright ballads and nature poems, and one well-known lyric, "Florence Vane."

C. HENRY B. TIMROD (1829–67) and PAUL HAMILTON HAYNE (1830–86), younger South Carolina friends of Simms.

  1. Timrod wrote sonnets and patriotic poems of considerable finish and force; cf. the war-time poems, "Charleston" (written 1861) and "The Cotton Boll."

  2. Hayne's verse was eloquent, sensuous, musical, but too facile; deserving of mention are "The Island in the South" (1859), "Aspects of the Pines" (1872), and "Unveiled" (1882), an ode to the Southern spirit of nature, in a vein between Wordsworth's and Shelley's.

III. Walt Whitman (1819–92)

A. Born on Long Island, May 31, 1819; printer, New York, school teacher, journalist, 1836–49; editor, *Brooklyn Daily Eagle*, 1848–49; traveled in South, West, and Canada; house builder, Brooklyn; first volume of poems, 1855; visiting army hospitals, 1863–65; government clerk; invalid, Camden, N.J., 1874–92; died March 26, 1892. Loved both nature and the life of towns; youth Bohemian and consciously violent and pagan; later years more restrained; somewhat indolent; some vulgarity; rather harmless egotism and affectation, with essential charm and sincerity.

B. Poems include *Leaves of Grass* (1855), republished with revisions and additions eight times to 1892; *Drum Taps* (1865); *Passage to India* (1871); etc. The prose works—*Democratic Vistas* (1871), *Specimen Days and Collect* (1882), *A Backward Glance o'er Travel'd Roads* (1888), etc.—supplement and illustrate the ideas of the poems.

C. Poems grouped by subjects
   1. Autobiographical poems
      a) Whitman's individual character, ideas, etc., as in "There Was a Child Went Forth"[1] (1855), glimpses of his childhood; "Song of the Open Road" (1856), comradeship in the observation of life; "Me Imperturbe" (1860); and three poems in which he forecasts the final separation of body and soul, whose unity was his recurrent theme—"Darest Thou Now, O Soul" (1871), "The Last Invocation" (1871), and "Good-Bye, My Fancy" (1891), his doubtful-hopeful adieu to life. See, also, "Full of Life Now" (1860), addressed to the posthumous reader; "Night on the Prairies" (1860) and "A Noiseless Patient Spider" (1871), meditations on the mystery of life; and "Yet, Yet, Ye Downcast Hours" (1870), asking, What after death?
      b) Whitman a representative human being; as in "Song of Myself"[2] (1855), "One's-Self I Sing" (1867), etc.
   2. Poems of democracy
      a) Aspiration toward democracy and illustration of it a favorite theme. Method of presentation (1) largely panoramic or enumerative, as in "Song of the Broad-Axe" (1856), "Crossing Brooklyn Ferry" (1856), "Starting from Paumanok" (1860), and "I Hear America Singing" (1860); or (2) in combination with interpretative comment, as in "As I Sat Alone by Blue Ontario's Shore" (1860); "Pioneers! O Pioneers!" (1865), a stirring expression of the spirit of the American pioneer; "For You, O Democracy" (1860), a sketch of his task of teaching comradeship; and "So Long!" (1860), a summary of what he has taught, and a picture of the free race that will come.

[1] The dates are of the first issue of each poem. In later editions there is much revision and expansion, and often change of title.

[2] In most of early editions called "Walt Whitman."

    b) The evolution of democracy to a world-wide unity, in the "unfolding of cosmic purposes," is the vision set forth in *Passage to India* (1871), a poem immediately inspired by the opening of the Suez Canal and the transcontinental railroad.

3. Poems of the war

    a) A series of brilliant etchings, some perfect, some too harsh, published in *Drum Taps* (1865); including "Cavalry Crossing a Ford," "By the Bivouac's Fitful Flame," "Vigil Strange I Kept on the Field One Night," "Come Up from the Fields, Father," and the autobiographical narrative, "The Dresser."

    b) Two splendid poems on Lincoln's death: "When Lilacs Last in the Dooryard Bloomed" (1865), and "O Captain! My Captain!" (1865).

4. Nature poetry

    a) Throughout the poems there are descriptive details of every kind; they show (1) great accuracy and wide range of observation, (2) directness and vividness, (3) delicacy and coarseness side by side.

    b) Distinct poems of nature not numerous, and limited in scope; concerned with nature's dramas and pageants, especially of sea, winds, mountains, and vast reaches of sky and plain.

        (1) Great emotional sweep in "Out of the Cradle Endlessly Rocking" (1859), "On the Beach at Night" (1871); "To the Man-of-War-Bird" (1876); and "With Husky-Haughty Lips, O Sea" (1884).

        (2) More restraint in "O Magnet-South" (1860), an enumerative description; "Give Me the Splendid Silent Sun" (1865), praising equally the rural and the urban scene; "Spirit that Form'd This Scene" (1881), asserting the kinship of his poetry and the wild and artless nature of the Rocky Mountains.

    c) Among the later works a few brief passages show a quiet or meditative enjoyment of nature, as, "The First Dandelion" (1888) and "A Prairie Sunset" (1888).

D. Whitman's central ideas

1. The Emersonian doctrine of self-dependence, which becomes vigorous self-assertion.

2. The significance of modern science, particularly the evolutionary point of view, and the rightness of everything natural.

3. Universal democracy as a goal, to be attained as the result of social evolution. America's destiny to advance by her example the long evolution of the race.

4. Democracy gives opportunity for developing larger and more vivid personalities; it finds fitting expression in comradeship based on the recognition of the equality of men.

E. Whitman's art

1. Though admiring the great poets of the past, he aims (a) to avoid the use of regular meter, rhyme, traditional metaphors, and allusions; (b) to be independent of the accepted canons of taste, in diction (cf. his slang and coinages) and in subjects; (c) to hit a new form which should be American, modern, natural, suited to his themes.

2. Literary relations

a) Whitman under the influence of "Ossian" and the rhapsodic passages of the Old Testament.

b) In turn exerted considerable influence on later versifiers, in matter of metrical freedom as well as freedom of speech.

F. General estimate

1. His rhythms often pronounced, sufficiently regular, and stirring; at times they degenerate into bald prose.

2. Frequent passages of high imaginative quality, but poetic continuity seldom sustained beyond the paragraph.

3. Certain large and fine ideas set forth with emotional intensity

4. No humor, taste often offensive, sentiment eccentric; but as he grows older, his ideas and his form move away from the extreme and coarse toward the normal.

5. Net impression produced is of naïve but powerful character, individual and essentially dignified, with a limited but genuine poetic endowment.

IV. Bayard Taylor (1825–78)

   A. A Pennsylvanian; made wandering tour of Europe, 1844–46; newspaper work, writing; extensive tours of Europe, Asia, Africa; lecturing; non-resident professor of German at Cornell; Minister to Germany; voluminous writer.

   B. Poems fluent, musical, somewhat sensuous; influenced by Shelley, and later by Tennyson.

    1. Dramas: *The Prophet* (1874), an unsuccessful treatment of Mormonism; *The Masque of the Gods* (1872) and *Prince Deukalion* (1878), Shelleyan allegories containing effective lyrical passages.

    2. Narrative poems, less ambitious but more successful, include *Lars: A Pastoral of Norway* (1873) and ballads of California and Pennsylvania life.

    3. Lyrics. His most famous poem the "Bedouin Song," in *Poems of the Orient* (1854), a volume which introduced the Orient into American literature, and represents him at his best

    4. Translation of Goethe's *Faust* (1870–71), considered his greatest work and the best translation by an American.

   C. Prose works. Numerous successful volumes of travels, some indifferent literary criticism, and four novels.

   D. Taylor a talented, versatile, cosmopolitan writer of the second rank.

V. Minor Poets of the Middle States

    Minor poets of the Middle States include THOMAS BUCHANAN REED (1822–72), author of "Sheridan's Ride" (1865); GEORGE HENRY BOKER* (1823–90), most famous as a dramatist, who wrote respectable lyrics and sonnets; CHARLES GODFREY LELAND (1824–1903), author of *Hans Breitman's Ballads* (collected edition, 1871) in humorous German-American dialect; and RICHARD HENRY STODDARD (1825–1903), who wrote, under the influence of Keats and others, skilful but commonplace poems, perhaps best represented in *Songs of Summer* (1857).

ESSAYS, CRITICISM, AND MISCELLANEOUS PROSE TO 1870

I. Washington Irving* (1783–1859)

   A. Born in New York, April 3, 1783; in Europe, 1804–6; admitted to New York bar, 1806; resident in Europe, 1815–32; LL.D..

Oxford, 1830; Secretary of United States Legation, England, 1830–31; returned to America, 1832; Minister to Spain, 1842–46; died November 28, 1859.

B. First American author to be recognized abroad, and one of the early links between European culture and traditions and American literature. Wrote under the influence of English prose writers of the eighteenth century and with a knowledge of the European scene.

C. Essays and sketches. Show kinship with, and probable influence of, Addison and Goldsmith. Graceful and entertaining; somewhat thin. Begin with the *Oldstyle* letters (1802) and *Salmagundi* (1807–8), a miscellany by Irving, his brother WILLIAM, and JAMES K. PAULDING.* *The Sketch Book* (1819–20), which brought him general fame, and *Bracebridge Hall* (1822) contain sketches of English and American scenes. *The Alhambra* (1832) is a book of Spanish sketches.

D. Tales. Published in the volumes of essays and sketches, and in *Tales of a Traveller* (1824). Irving's popular reputation rests mainly on "Rip Van Winkle," "The Legend of Sleepy Hollow," "The Stout Gentleman," etc.[1]

E. Descriptions of life in the West. Have some value as information and are in Irving's pleasant style; but not powerful, and largely done at second hand. The best are *A Tour on the Prairies* (1835) and *Astoria* (1836).

F. Biographies and histories
  1. Good literary histories, true to atmosphere and character, though not scholarly in the modern scientific sense.
  2. Titles: *The Life of Columbus* (1828), *The Conquest of Granada* (1829), said to be Irving's favorite, *Oliver Goldsmith* (1849), an admirable account of a kindred spirit, *Mahomet and His Successors* (1849–50), and *The Life of George Washington* (5 vols., 1855–59), superior to all previous presentations of Washington's character and not entirely superseded today.
  3. Here also may be placed his first success, the still amusing burlesque *Knickerbocker's History of New York* (1809).

[1] Cf. above, p. 21.

G. General estimate
1. No great creative power, or force or vigor or subtlety of mind.
2. Command of humor, graceful fancy, kindly satire, luminous style; wide acquaintance with European culture. Historically an important figure, and still beloved.

II. The Transcendentalists
A. Transcendentalism
1. Origins and relations: the special New England form of a general movement.
   a) European parallels: (1) in politics—the French Revolution; (2) in philosophy—the Kantean idealistic attack on the "sensational" materialism of Locke; (3) in literature—the Romantic revolt against tradition, laws, conventions.
   b) American precursors: (1) in politics—the American Revolution; (2) in religion—the Unitarian movement toward a liberal Christianity, as against the rigid Calvinism of the church as late as Jonathan Edwards (1703–58): in 1785 King's Chapel, Boston, revised its liturgy along Unitarian lines; in 1815 the name "Unitarian" adopted; CHANNING's* sermon at Baltimore in 1819 provides the link between Unitarianism and Transcendentalism.
2. What Transcendentalism meant
   a) Specifically means "idealism"; "transcendental" applied to what "transcends" experience: philosophically, the belief in innate, intuitive knowledge, as of God or Truth; in New England fundamentally a philosophical and religious conception, best expounded in Emerson's *Nature* (1836).
   b) The term also used more generally—as in Europe "Romanticism" covers many diverse expressions of the desire for freedom—to include various forms of revolt against the rationalistic, the traditional, the conventional, the fettered; as appears in the lives and interests of the chief Transcendentalists.
   c) Like the cognate European movements, (1) it had value as revolt, as idealism, and for practical reforms it promoted; (2) it had defects of nebulousness and extravagance.

3. Immediate inspiration to Transcendentalism: (1) the quiet development of local tendencies—i.e., Unitarianism and the political revolution; (2) contact with foreign thought, especially the German philosophy of Kant, Schelling, etc., by way of Coleridge, Carlyle, and the poetry of Wordsworth; (3) the native character of individuals, as in the case of Emerson.

4. Dates in the transcendental movement: 1832, Emerson resigns his pastorate because unwilling to administer the rite of the Lord's Supper; visits England, and meets Coleridge, Wordsworth, Carlyle; 1836, Emerson's *Nature*; 1836, Transcendental Club founded; 1837, Emerson's *American Scholar*, and 1838, Emerson's *Divinity School Address*, called Declarations of Independence for American letters and religion, respectively; 1840–44, *The Dial;* 1841–47, the Brook Farm experiment.

B. Minor Transcendentalists

1. Amos Bronson Alcott (1799–1888), eccentric, mystical, extreme; taught school in accordance with radical theories; held public "conversations"; established the Concord School of Philosophy. Father of Louisa M. Alcott.

2. George Ripley (1802–80), a Unitarian minister; active in the Brook Farm venture; assistant editor of *The Dial;* literary editor, *New York Tribune.*

3. Sarah Margaret Fuller (1810–50), of striking personality and great intellectual force; best illustrates the literary-cultural side of Transcendentalism; edited *The Dial*, which contained philosophical discussions, papers on foreign literature, etc.; critic for *New York Tribune;* social worker; married Marquis Ossoli, 1847; author of *Woman in the Nineteenth Century* (1844) and *Papers on Literature and Art* (1846).

4. Among others more or less intimately associated with Transcendentalism are: James Freeman Clarke (1810–88), Unitarian minister, abolitionist, author; Theodore Parker* (1810–60), radical Unitarian minister, abolitionist; Jones Very (1813–80), Unitarian minister, mystical poet; also William Henry Channing, Christopher P. Cranch, George William Curtis,* Charles A. Dana, and Hawthorne.*

C. RALPH WALDO EMERSON* (1803–82)

1. The most important of the Transcendentalists, though not an active sharer in their group activities; in his prose he phrases most adequately the Transcendental philosophy.

2. Chief works in prose are: *Nature* (1836); *Essays* (1st series, 1841; 2d series, 1844), based upon his public lectures, among them "The Over-Soul," "Self-Reliance," "Compensation," "History," "Friendship"; *Representative Men* (1850), from lectures in London; the acute *English Traits* (1856); *The Conduct of Life* (1860). His *Journals* (10 vols., 1909–14) are an important contribution to the understanding of his life as man, author, and philosopher.

3. His thought

   a) Essentially expressed in *Nature*, all his work an amplification or illustration of a few central ideas.

      (1) The spiritual the only reality; man's better nature, the Over-soul, a part of the Infinite, of Deity; God the unifying principle of all existence.

      (2) We must give scope to the Over-soul by developing self-reliance.

      (3) We should approach the practical issues of life more ideally.

   b) Besides general philosophical views, his writings contain scores of shrewd practical maxims for the individual life.

4. General estimate

   a) Great magnetism and power to inspire; purity, keenness, charm.

   b) Provinciality; insufficient recognition of the problem of evil; remoteness from the contacts of ordinary life.

   c) Ideas intuitional, "flashes of insight," not ordered, documented, demonstrated; hence, effect of incoherence or obscurity, sentiments lofty, somewhat elusive, and too often repeated.

   d) Constant brilliancy of individual utterances, as in the poems; phrasing of truths which come home.

D. HENRY DAVID THOREAU (1817–62)

1. Born in Concord, July 12, 1817; graduated at Harvard, 1837; school teacher, pencil maker (with his father), land surveyor;

lived with Emerson, 1841–43; lived alone at Walden Pond, 1845–47; died, May 5, 1862. An individualist, rebellious against authority of Church or State; abolitionist; original devotee of the simple life; naturalist and transcendental philosopher.

2. Works

  a) Some poems in the Emersonian vein, but feebler.

  b) Numerous magazine articles.

  c) Books published during his life; unsuccessful at the time.

  (1) *A Week on the Concord and Merrimac Rivers* (1849); a combination of narrative with descriptions of nature and people and philosophical discourses; shows some influence of Emerson and Carlyle, but has original flavor; weak construction but admirable style.

  (2) *Walden* (1854), his best and most characteristic book; an absorbing account of his two years as a "hermit," interrupted, like the narrative in *A Week*, etc., by philosophy and description.

  d) Posthumous works include: *Excursions* (1863), containing admirable nature sketches; *The Maine Woods* (1864); *Early Spring in Massachusetts* (1881); etc.

3. General estimate

  a) Thoreau's personality gives character to the works: marked by delicacy, homeliness, humor; intimacy of knowledge of outer nature; shrewd estimates of life.

  b) Some eccentricity, extravagance, tediousness, diffuseness.

  c) Two styles, "the oracular and the simple," the former sometimes ludicrous, the latter charming.

III. Oliver Wendell Holmes* (1809–94)

A. Though no more characteristic of him than his poems or his novels, Holmes's essays perhaps allow the most perfect expression, in most congenial form, of his special gifts. In essays as in poetry appears his kinship with the brilliant, witty, and genial spirits of the eighteenth century; also, the influence of his scientific training.

B. Miscellaneous essays, chiefly medical in theme, but often of considerable general interest.

    1. *Homœopathy, and its Kindred Delusions* (1842) and *The Contagiousness of Puerperal Fever* (1843), two famous essays; reprinted, with others (1861); again reprinted, with later essays, in *Medical Essays* (1883).

    2. *Soundings from the Atlantic* (1863), general essays collected from the *Atlantic Monthly; Pages from an Old Volume of Life. A Collection of Essays . . . . 1857–1881* (1883).

C. The "Autocrat Series." Brilliant conversational essays, in the form of "table talk," begun in first volume of the *Atlantic* and continued in later volumes. Won instant recognition in America and abroad, for wit, observation of human nature, kindliness, shrewdness, wide if not deep philosophy; discursive, yet with a sufficient unity in the tone, helped by the personality of the dominating "Autocrat"; the crystallized conversation of "one of the most brilliant talkers that ever lived."

    1. *The Autocrat of the Breakfast Table* (1858), first, most spontaneous, most original of the series; talk about the table by a group, all sufficiently sketched but present wholly to provide an audience for the Autocrat.

    2. *The Professor at the Breakfast Table* (1859) continues the talk with slightly less brilliancy, slightly more story. As "professor" (of anatomy) the Autocrat is essentially unchanged.

    3. *The Poet at the Breakfast Table* (1872) completes the slight love story hinted at in the previous volumes. As "poet" the Autocrat introduces various verses to his submissive companions.

    4. *Over the Tea Cups* (1890), aptly named, is still excellent talk with something of the quieter wisdom of age.

D. Biographical and autobiographical works

    1. *John Lothrop Motley. A Memoir* (1878), well written, an eloquent defense by an intimate friend; not a penetrating interpretation of his importance as a literary historian.

    2. *Life of Ralph Waldo Emerson* in "American Men of Letters Series" (1884), well planned, appreciative, and very happily phrased; a not wholly successful portrait of a very different type of man from himself.

    3. *Our Hundred Days in Europe* (1887) is a charming narrative of his last foreign voyage.

IV. Lesser Writers of the Literary Essay

    A. Reflections of European travel; cultivated, somewhat self-consciously so at times

        1. LONGFELLOW'S *Outre-Mer* (1833–34), EMERSON'S *English Traits* (1856), HAWTHORNE'S *Our Old Home* (1863) have already been mentioned.

        2. NATHANIEL PARKER WILLIS* (1806–67): *Pencillings by the Way* (1844) and *Letters from under a Bridge* (1844).

        3. DONALD G. MITCHELL, "Ik Marvel" (1822–1908), gave his first book the significant title, *Fresh Gleanings; or, A New Sheaf from the Old Fields of Continental Europe* (1847).

        4. BAYARD TAYLOR* (1825–78) was the author of many entertaining books of travel, *The Lands of the Saracen* (1854), *A Visit to India, China, and Japan* (1855), *Northern Travel* (1857), etc.

        5. GEORGE WILLIAM CURTIS* (1824–92) in *Nile Notes of a Howadji* (1851) and *The Howadji in Syria* (1852) added distinction to the familiar vehicle by the light humor and grace of his style.

    B. The narrative-meditative sketch becomes a book in

        1. The soberly sentimental *Reveries of a Bachelor* (1850) and *Dream Life* (1851) of DONALD G. MITCHELL and

        2. The witty and playfully sentimental *Prue and I* (1856) of GEORGE WILLIAM CURTIS.*

V. Critics

    A. EDGAR ALLAN POE* (1809–49)

        1. Criticism before Poe mostly confined to magazine reviews and negligible in character.

        2. Along with much hack work Poe produced some excellent criticism, including

            a) Famous reviews of Longfellow's *Ballads* (1842), Hawthorne's *Twice-Told Tales* (1842), Dickens' *Barnaby Rudge*, etc.

            b) Critical essays, including *The Rationale of Verse* (1848) and *The Poetic Principle* (1850), containing his definition of poetry as "the rhythmic creation of beauty."

            c) *Marginalia*, critical notes collected from magazines.

        3. Qualities of his criticism

a) Comments often acute and just, because of his keen, analytical intellect, experience as an artist in prose and verse, courage in praising and condemning.

b) Weaknesses: narrow range of knowledge of literature; too great emphasis on technique; special foibles, as for originality, unity, and freedom from the didactic.

c) His independence of utterance and purely artistic point of view highly useful at the time.

B. JAMES RUSSELL LOWELL* (1819-91)

1. Lowell's combination of the rôles of poet, critic, general essayist, and scholar gives him a position in American literature comparable to that of Arnold in English literature.

2. Chief prose works

a) Essays mainly critical: *Conversations on Some of the Old Poets* (1845); *Among My Books* (1st series, 1870; 2d series, 1876), including essays on Dryden, Dante, Spenser, Milton, Shakspere, etc.; *My Study Windows* (1871), including essays on Carlyle, Thoreau, Chaucer, etc.

b) Miscellaneous essays: *Fireside Travels* (1864); "On a Certain Condescension in Foreigners," etc. (in *My Study Windows* 1871); *Democracy and Other Addresses* (1887); etc.

c) His *Letters* (1893) are delightful.

3. Character of his criticism

a) Subjects: mainly the greater writers whom he loves and can eulogize.

b) Strength: equipment of sound catholic taste, extremely wide reading, sound scholarship; vigorous good sense, penetration, sympathy, humor, richness of thought and feeling; urbane and often vigorous and witty style; happy poetic metaphors.

c) Defects: lack of philosophical interest; disinclination to close and searching analysis; absence of central controlling ideas, which produces effect of weak structure, lack of concentration, defective emphasis.

VI. Orators

A. Clergymen. Most important are: WILLIAM ELLERY CHANNING* (1780-1842), author of the historically important sermon, *Uni-*

tarian Christianity (1819), and THEODORE PARKER* (1810–60), Unitarians; and HENRY WARD BEECHER (1813–87), the most impressive pulpit orator of his time, author of the famous fighting *Liverpool Address* (1863) in defense of the Northern cause, various volumes of sermons and addresses, and one indifferent novel.

B. Political orators

1. JOHN C. CALHOUN (1782–1850), of South Carolina, became the chief defender of state sovereignty, and of the right of nullification of federal laws and of secession; possessed of extraordinary logical acuteness and adroitness.

2. HENRY CLAY (1777–1852), of Kentucky; skilful advocate of compromise; speaker of great personal charm; work of small literary value.

3. DANIEL WEBSTER (1782–1852)

   a) Born in New Hampshire; graduated at Dartmouth, 1801; Representative in Congress, 1813–15, 1823–27; Senator from Massachusetts, 1827–41, 1845–52; Secretary of State, 1841–43. Greatest American orator; impressive personality, tremendous popularity in New England until the supposed apostasy of his seventh of March speech favoring compromise with the South.

   b) Chief orations are: Dartmouth College case (1818); Plymouth oration (1820); address at the laying of the cornerstone of Bunker Hill Monument (1825); funeral oration on Adams and Jefferson (1826); reply to Hayne (1830); argument in the White murder case (1830); address at the completion of Bunker Hill Monument (1843); seventh of March speech (1850).

   c) Manner eloquent, stately, of a type now thought old-fashioned, with passion and emotional appeal. Somewhat lacking in literary and cultural background, and in range of interests.

4. ABRAHAM LINCOLN (1809–65), not an orator in the strict sense; characterized by great keenness of mind, ability to grasp essentials, earnestness, directness, loftiness of character, a biblical simplicity and elevation of style. Exhibited in debates with STEPHEN A. DOUGLAS (1860) and *Cooper Union Address* (1860)

during his first presidential campaign, in his first and his second *Inaugural* (1861, 1865), and especially in his brief masterpiece, the *Gettysburg Address* (1863).

5. WENDELL PHILLIPS (1811–84), Harvard graduate abolitionist, radical; flaming orator of high principle and extraordinary fascination, but extravagant and specious. Most famous speeches: the eulogy, *Toussaint l'Ouverture*, on the "black Washington" of Haiti (1861); and *The Scholar in a Republic* (1881), a sensational attack on the college man as citizen, before the Harvard Phi Beta Kappa.

C. Literary and academic orators include: EDWARD EVERETT (1794–1865), a most finished speaker, constantly in demand for occasional addresses; GEORGE WILLIAM CURTIS* (1824–92), editor, publicist, author of many graceful eulogies and occasional addresses, among them *The Puritan Principle: Liberty under the Law* (1876), *The Leadership of Educated Men* (1882), and *Wendell Phillips* (1884).

VII. Historians

A. Miscellaneous writers

1. Subjects: the Revolution, state history, general history of the United States.

2. Method increasingly scientific and accurate; manner for the most part unliterary.

3. Representative names are: JOHN MARSHALL, author of *Life of Washington* (1804–7); Mrs. MERCY OTIS WARREN,* author of *History of the American Revolution* (3 vols., 1805); RICHARD HILDRETH (1807–65), author of a substantial, dull *History of the United States* (6 vols., 1849–52); and GEORGE BANCROFT (1800–1891), student in Germany, Secretary of the Navy, Minister to England, who wrote a minute, painstaking, rhetorical, and ponderous *History of the United States* (12 vols., 1834–82; revised, 6 vols., 1883–85).

B. Literary historians

1. WILLIAM HICKLING PRESCOTT (1796–1859), in his *Ferdinand and Isabella* (1837), *The Conquest of Mexico* (1843) and *The Conquest of Peru* (1847), presented the results of conscientious research

with finish, dignity, and vividness; acclaimed and honored abroad; still read, though superseded as a historian.

2. JOHN LOTHROP MOTLEY (1814–77), Minister to Austria and England, also received notable foreign recognition for his brilliant, vivid, somewhat partisan *Rise of the Dutch Republic* (1856), *History of the United Netherlands* (1860–68), etc.

3. FRANCIS PARKMAN (1823–93), most successful in combining fidelity to the facts of history with literary color and charm of style. Among his best works are: *The California and Oregon Trail* (1849), *Pioneers of France in the New World* (1865), *The Old Régime in Canada* (1874), and *Montcalm and Wolfe* (1884).

THE LITERATURE FROM 1870 TO THE WORLD WAR

GENERAL TENDENCIES

I. Changes in American Life

A. Politically: From a small nation of 38,000,000 (1870), sectionally divided, in a country largely undeveloped, the United States has grown to be the richest and most powerful of nations, unified by three wars, in spite of the influx of millions of immigrants who have helped to swell the population to over 100,000,000.

B. Socially: Increase of wealth, rise of standard of living, development of class feeling and industrial warfare, economic unrest.

C. Spiritually: Partly by reason of more adequate and general education, there is less provincialism; greater liberalism in the conceptions of religion, conduct, literature, and art; keener sense of civic and social responsibility.

D. America today for the first time out of her isolation; pretty completely a part of the complex, confused, struggling, aspiring modern world.

I. Currents in American Literature

A. Fifty years with no "formula," a transitional time; geographically decentralized with the passing of the New England group; few commanding figures, but much significant experimentation. Distinct technical advance in short story, novel, and drama. In subjects the works are more definitely American, and present with increasing freedom all phases of individual and social life.

B. Dominant moods and tendencies
  1. Romance and sentimentalism, leaning hard on traditional fashions, 1860–80, with a swing toward realistic portrayal of local conditions of life, "local color," in the seventies.
  2. A quiet, reticent realism in the eighties.
  3. A sharper, harsher, rebellious realism beginning in the nineties.
  4. A return to high-colored romance, largely historical, for a decade from the middle nineties.

5. In the last fifteen years a great variety of work: (1) the romantic —return to nature, the primitive, gentle vagabondage, crime, big business, etc.; (2) the quietly realistic; but particularly, (3) an increasing literature, outgrowth in part of the harsh realism of the nineties, which strikes the note of revolt and experimentation, (a) in form—shapeless "raw materials" novels, "new" poetry, one-act plays—and (b) in naturalism, a frank or brutal realism of subject and treatment.

THE NOVEL

I. Transitional Writers

A. EDWARD PAYSON ROE (1838–88), a clergyman, wrote many novels, containing an extremely popular blend of sentiment, moralizing, and sensationalism, beginning with *Barriers Burned Away* (1872).

B. EDWARD EGGLESTON (1837–1902), also a clergyman and a moralist, was a pioneer realist, portraying interestingly and simply Middle-Western backwoods life in *The Hoosier School-Master* (1871), *The Circuit Rider* (1874), *Roxy* (1878), *The Graysons* (1888), etc.

C. LEWIS WALLACE (1827–1905) wrote high-colored romances, *The Fair God* (1873), a tale of the conquest of Mexico; *Ben-Hur, a Tale of the Christ* (1880), still somewhat popular; and *The Prince of India* (1893).

D. FRANCES HODGSON BURNETT (1849–1924) though much of her work falls in and shows influence of a later time, belongs here for the combined sentimentalism and realism of her early successes, *That Lass o' Lowrie's* (1877), *Little Lord Fauntleroy* (1886), and *Sara Crewe* (1888).

II. Samuel Langhorne Clemens, "Mark Twain" (1835–1910)

A. Born in Florida, Mo., November 30, 1835; common-school education; printer in New York, etc.; Mississippi River pilot, 1858–61; mining and newspaper work, Nevada and California; lecturing; first trip to Europe, 1867; Litt.D., Oxford, 1907; died April 21, 1910. Like Whitman, an outspoken, robustious American; close to "the people," product of the rough freedom of the new West; temperamental, vigorous, radical; superficially a jester, but with an undercurrent of seriousness and pessimism; perhaps the most loved and most "American" author of his time.

B. Literary relations

   1. Antagonistic to the traditional culture of New England and its literary representatives; dislike of Hawthorne, Henry James, Scott, Jane Austen, etc.

   2. Heir to the devices of the earlier American humorists, who chiefly practiced a "gigantic exaggeration and calm-faced mendacity"—GEORGE H. DERBY, "John Phoenix" (1823–61) HENRY WHEELER SHAW, "Josh Billings" (1818–85), DAVID ROSS LOCKE, "Petroleum V. Nasby" (1833–88), and CHARLES FARRAR BROWNE, "Artemas Ward" (1834–67); also influenced by Bret Harte and coached somewhat by his friend, William Dean Howells.

C. Narratives of Western life

   1. *Roughing It* (1873), a semi-autobiographical account of a trip through the far West, and *Life on the Mississippi* (1883; in part published as *Old Times on the Mississippi, Atlantic Monthly,* 1875), though not novels, show his essential characteristics; both full of intimate knowledge of place and time, vivid, graphic, humorous narratives, with epic sweep.

   2. *The Gilded Age* (1873), written in collaboration with CHARLES DUDLEY WARNER,* his first novel, though ill-constructed and uneven, is memorable for its picture of a mushroom town and for the character of Colonel Sellers.

   3. *The Adventures of Tom Sawyer* (1876) and its sequel, *The Adventures of Huckleberry Finn* (1884), two of the greatest stories of boys, represent: (1) realism as against moral Sunday-school tales, (2) understanding of boy nature, (3) splendid, easy narrative. *Huckleberry Finn*, with its epical view of the life along the great river and its unity of tone and construction, is perhaps his greatest work.

D. Narratives with a European background

   1. Books of travel

      a) *The Innocents Abroad* (1869) sensationally introduced him to literary America and Europe; a mixture of seriousness and cheap jocosity; much rather blatant and silly Americanism; long a very popular book, partly by virtue of its faults.

 b) *A Tramp Abroad* (1880), on a walking tour of the Alps.

 2. *The Prince and the Pauper* (1881), a historical romance for children, *A Connecticut Yankee in King Arthur's Court* (1889), with its splendid narrative power, its extraordinary comic incongruities, and its savage satire, and *Personal Recollections of Joan of Arc* (1896), a moving idealization of Joan's career, all reveal his hatred of oppression political, ecclesiastical, or social.

 3. *The Mysterious Stranger* (1916; written in 1898), in the visit of "Satan" to the boys of a sixteenth-century Austrian village, phrases with dramatic skill the agnostic pessimism of his later years; cf., also, *What Is Man?* (1906; written 1898) and *Captain Stormfield's Visit to Heaven* (1908).

E. Among minor stories and miscellaneous works are: "The Jumping Frog of Calaveras County" (1867), *Pudd'nhead Wilson* (1894), *The American Claimant* (1892), *Following the Equator* (1897), *The Man that Corrupted Hadleyburg* (1899), *A Double-Barrelled Detective Story* (1902).

F. General estimate

 1. Master of graphic narrative of a simple, masculine type, with unforced reality of scene and characters.

 2. Style and construction those of the improviser, often happy, too often rough and crude.

 3. A great-hearted American and radical democrat, of noble earnestness but violent prejudices.

 4. A great humorist, of the uproarious rather than the subtle type.

III. William Dean Howells* (1837–1920)

A. Born in Ohio, March 1, 1837; common-school education; printer, newspaper correspondent, and editor, Ohio; Consul at Venice, 1861–65; newspaper work; editor, *Atlantic Monthly*, 1872–81; abroad, 1881–85; on staff, *Harper's Magazine*, 1885–1920; Litt.D., Oxford, 1904; died May 11, 1920. Versatile, copious, and finished novelist; also poet, dramatist, critic, and essavist.

B. Literary relations

    1. Steeped in the best literary traditions, early admiring Chaucer, Macaulay, Hawthorne, and Heine; later Jane Austen, Turgenev, Tolstoi.

    2. Acknowledged leader in the movement toward realism, through precept and example; dominating more than two decades with his prolific pen; followed by many, provoking others to a fiercer truth.

C. Novels of his Boston period. Concerned chiefly with manners, the clash of individual temperaments; materials drawn, in accordance with his theory of realism, from average life, the normal, approaching the commonplace. Beginning lightly, gracefully, they steadily increase in scope and power; all technically skilful. Among the best are

    1. *A Chance Acquaintance* (1873), his first novel with a plot, a study in snobbishness which separates two lovers; social conflicts and contrasts in *A Foregone Conclusion* (1875), *The Lady of the Aroostook* (1879), *A Fearful Reponsibility*, a long short story (1881), and *Dr. Breen's Practice* (1881).

    2. The period culminates in three admirable novels: *A Modern Instance* (1882), most powerful of all, containing his finest heroine, Marcia Gaylord, and the masterly portrait of her unworthy husband, Bartley Hubbard; *The Rise of Silas Lapham* (1884), story of an honest, crude self-made man and his family struggling to adapt themselves to a cultivated environment; and the graceful comedy, *Indian Summer* (1885), which Howells thought his best, narrating with kindly, humorous wisdom the experience of a middle-aged lover.

D. Novels of his New York period. The clashes in the situations now less personal, more social; wider interest, promoted by reading of Tolstoi, in industrial, political, and religious problems; yet the novels show unflagging urbanity and ease, though some lessening of power.

    1. *A Hazard of New Fortunes* (1889), broader in canvas, with New York as the scene and a great variety of distinctly drawn characters, is among his most successful studies.

2. *The Kentons* (1902) is an excellent example of his later penetrating, but still well-poised, realism.

3. *A Traveler from Altruria* (1894) and *Through the Eye of the Needle* (1907) are Utopian romances.

4. *The Shadow of a Dream* (1890) and his last novel, *The Leatherwood God* (1916), illustrate his handling of the problem of the relation of this world to the spiritual world; cf., also, his early unsympathetic treatment of spiritualism in *The Undiscovered Country* (1880).

5. Among others are: *An Imperative Duty* (1891), *The Quality of Mercy* (1892), *The World of Chance* (1893), *The Landlord of Lion's Head* (1897), and *The Son of Royal Langbrith* (1904).

E. General estimate

1. Author of half a dozen admirable novels and of many nearly flawless in technique; none quite a masterpiece in depth or power; yet distinguished for the volume, representativeness, finish, and wise humanity of his work.

2. Technical methods simple yet masterly; style inconspicuously felicitous and graceful.

3. Limitation chiefly in the "selective" character of his realism— his unwillingness to deal directly with the problems presented by the sin and vice in the world.

IV. Henry James* (1843–1916)

A. Born in New York City, April 15, 1843, son of Henry James, Sr., and brother of William James, the philosopher; private schooling at home and abroad, followed by study at Harvard Law School; nearly all his life resident abroad, mainly in England; became a British subject in 1915; died February 28, 1916. Author of novels, short stories, plays, books of travel, criticism, and autobiography.

B. Literary relations

1. Youthful experimenting, chiefly in the short story, encouraged by Charles Eliot Norton and Howells, shows influence of Hawthorne, and perhaps of George Eliot.

2. Later dominating influences were Flaubert, Balzac, but chiefly Turgenev.

C. Novels of his first period, 1875–90
   1. Chief theme the contrast provided by the simple, crude American
      in a sophisticated European setting; handled in part satirically,
      but with subtle understanding and with essential esteem for the
      American's superior integrity; plots not submerged, but never
      primary and often tenuous; style of classical finish and clarity.
   2. *Roderick Hudson* (1875), an unplausible story of the failure of a
      young American sculptor; *The American* (1877), the moral
      triumph of an American business man scorned by the family
      of the French girl he loves; *The Europeans* (1878), which exhibits
      the familiar contrast with the characters and scene reversed;
      and the short idyls of American girlhood, *Daisy Miller* (1879)
      and *An International Episode* (1879)—all precede and prepare
      for his first great novel, *The Portrait of a Lady* (1881), with its
      European background rich in tradition, its charming heroine,
      and its close unity of plot and tone secured by his characteristic
      device of action viewed through the heroine's personality.
   3. Departure from the international theme in *The Bostonians*
      (1886), a harsh satire on feminism in America; *The Princess
      Cassamassima* (1886), with action centered in a group of revolu-
      tionists; and *The Tragic Muse* (1890), a plea for the rights of
      the artistic temperament.
D. The years 1890–95 spent in writing unsuccessful plays and some
   striking short stories, such as *The Lesson of the Master* (1892)
   and *The Altar of the Dead* (1895).
E. The later period, 1896–1917
   1. Characteristic differences: (*a*) increased concentration and a
      unity akin to that of the later short story but more intricate,
      obtained by suppressing the usual progressive action, avoiding
      drama, and instead unfolding a central situation, often through
      speculative analysis by a subsidiary character; (*b*) an increas-
      ingly complex style, the necessary vehicle for the intellectual
      subtleties of the analysis.
   2. The technically skilful *Spoils of Poynton* (1897), the terrible,
      pathetic, and most adroit contrast, in *What Maisie Knew* (1897),
      of childish innocence and multiple adulteries, and the unconscious
      parody of his own artifices in *The Awkward Age* (1899) are

succeeded by three great triumphs of his peculiar powers in *The Wings of the Dove* (1902), *The Ambassadors* (1903), called his best-constructed novel, and *The Golden Bowl* (1904).

3. Work of his remaining years scattered and fragmentary: two novels, *The Sense of the Past* and *The Ivory Tower*, left unfinished at his death (published 1917).

F. General estimate

1. A great realist in a restricted field; so restricted as to alienate most readers.

2. A great artist in perfection of structure, in precision and beauty of style, in power to create atmosphere; but extremely subtle and minute.

3. Dislike of the obvious, and remoteness from the ordinary activities and struggles of life.

V. Edith Wharton (1862–1937)

A. Born in New York City; married Edward Wharton, 1885; largely resident abroad; Chevalier of the Legion of Honor of France and of Leopold of Belgium.

B. At first strongly influenced by Henry James, and by Balzac and other Continental realists; began with short stories portraying a cosmopolitan society, often European, artistic-literary groups; later chiefly occupied with the novel.

C. A historical romance of Italy in the days of the French Revolution, *The Valley of Decision* (1902), shows lack of mastery of the novel form but has distinction of style and great richness of background.

D. Novels of social satire

1. *The House of Mirth* (1905), her first great success, portrays the world of fashion, with Lily Bart, a social parasite yet a pitiful and affecting figure, its victim.

2. *The Custom of the Country* (1913) is a stinging, rather depressing, satire on vulgar social "climbers" and on the "custom" of divorce, which is also the theme of *The Children* (1928).

3. *The Age of Innocence* (1921) is a masterly study of social life in New York in the seventies and its code of reticent "morality," of which the chief characters are the products and the victims.

E. Novels of human crises: less satirical, but equally subtle in analysis, particularly of passion; greater range and warmth of feeling.

    1. *The Fruit of the Tree* (1907), study of the alienation of husband and wife, with industrial problems in the background.

    2. *Ethan Frome* (1911), brief, poignant, stern; story of the agony of repressed love, in a tone of tragic irony, against the bleak background of New England snow-clad hills.

    3. *The Reef* (1912), of an intense love nearly shipwrecked by an impulsive infidelity; powerful analysis of the characters in their reactions to the situation.

    4. *Summer* (1917), an uncompromising picture of drunkenness and degeneracy in New England, out of which one character is lifted by the strength of his love.

    5. *The Glimpses of the Moon* (1922) presents the social parasite, as did *The House of Mirth*, but with more human warmth, if less satirical trenchancy.

    6. *Hudson River Bracketed* (1929) and its sequel, *The Gods Arrive* (1932), are primarily a study of the artistic temperament in conflict with or adjustment to environment.

F. General estimate

    1. Early work clever, sensitive, slightly "precious"; all her writing fine rather than robust, deriving power from disciplined intelligence rather than from naïve passion.

    2. The greatest contemporary master of fiction, for
        a) Structural symmetry and economy: style of exquisite simplicity, poise, and flexibility, at the same time reticent and subtle.
        b) Intimate knowledge of social milieus; powerful analysis of character; trenchant satire; intense feeling.

VI. Lesser Novelists

A. Entertainers

    1. FRANK R. [Francis Richard] STOCKTON (1834–1902)
        a) Began as writer of tales for children; editorial work on *Century* and *St. Nicholas* for many years. Distinguished for whimsical, wholesome humor, an extremely clever invention in the field of the unexpected and fantastic, tone of calm veracity, with abundance of realistic detail; characters

delightful, in naturalness often in comic contrast to their circumstances.

b) Among his better novels are: *Rudder Grange* (1879), his first great success; *The Casting Away of Mrs. Lecks and Mrs. Aleshine* (1886) and its sequel, *The Dusantes* (1888), comic tales of shipwreck and snowslide; *The Late Mrs. Null* (1886), a combination of ludicrous plot and charming, lifelike characters; *The Adventures of Captain Horn* (1895), a buried treasure story, and its sequel, *Mrs. Cliff's Yacht* (1896), in which a ship manned by clergymen fights pirates.

2. FRANCIS MARION CRAWFORD (1854-1909), born and nearly all his life resident in Italy, wrote many popular novels of dash and sparkle, easy in style, truthful in characters and setting, but of melodramatic plot and never deep or strong. The most successful deal with Italian themes, as, *A Roman Singer* (1884), *Saracinesca* (1887), *The Children of the King* (1893), and *Pietro Ghisleri* (1893).

B. Portrayers of local scenes and characters. Field chiefly belongs to the short story, but to a considerable extent represented in the novel.

1. New England .

    a) Short story writers who also wrote "local color" novels include: SARAH ORNE JEWETT* (1849-1909), in *A Country Doctor* (1884), etc.; MARY E. WILKINS FREEMAN* (1862-1930), in *Jerome, a Poor Young Man* (1897), etc.

    b) LOUISA M. ALCOTT (1832-88), author of a famous series of novels for children, *Little Women* (1868), *Little Men* (1871), etc., faithful pictures of real people.

2. New York provides the scene for HENRY CUYLER BUNNER* (1855-96) in *The Midge* (1886) and *The Story of a New York House* (1887), graceful and tender stories of New York City, HAROLD FREDERIC (1856-98) in *Seth's Brother's Wife* (1887); and EDWARD NOYES WESTCOTT (1847-98) in his study of a rural character, *David Harum* (1898); STEPHEN CRANE* (1871-1900), who helped to promote the newer, consciously outspoken realism in *Maggie: A Girl of the Streets* (copyrighted 1893; published 1896), but whose fame rests chiefly on *The Red Badge of Courage* (1895), study of the emotions of a raw recruit in the Civil War.

3. The South.   The most fertile field for the novel of local coloring, which is here generally romantic in tone.

   a) GEORGE W CABLE* (1844–1925) in *The Grandissimes* (1880) presents Creole life in Louisiana, and F HOPKINSON SMITH (1838–1915) in *Colonel Carter of Cartersville* (1891) and THOMAS NELSON PAGE* (1853–1922) in *Red Rock* (1898) present Virginia life, with intimacy and charm.

   b) Among others are: CONSTANCE FENIMORE WOOLSON (1848–94), in *East Angels* (1886), etc.; MARY N. MURFREE, "Charles Egbert Craddock" (1850–1922), in picturesque Tennessee narratives, including *The Prophet of the Great Smoky Mountains* (1885); the Kentucky writers, JAMES LANE ALLEN (1849–1925) in *The Choir Invisible* (1897), *The Reign of Law* (1900), etc., and JOHN FOX, JR. (1863–1919) in *The Little Shepherd of Kingdom Come* (1903), etc.

4. The Middle and Far West

   a) Quiet realism, sometimes mingled with romance: MARY HALLOCK FOOTE (1847–1938), author of *The Led-Horse Claim* (1883), *The Chosen Valley* (1892), etc., California stories in the vein of Bret Harte; BOOTH TARKINGTON (1869–   ), author of *The Gentleman from Indiana* (1899), *The Conquest of Canaan* (1905), *The Turmoil* (1915), *The Plutocrat* (1927), and studies of youth in *Penrod* (1914) and *Alice Adams* (1921); OWEN WISTER (1860–1938), author of *The Virginian* (1902), a "Wild West" story with a literary coloring.

   b) Harsh and grim realism, often combined with attack on social and other abuses

     (1) EDGAR W. HOWE (1853–1937), whose *The Story of a Country Town* (1883) is called the sternest of American novels.

     (2) FRANK NORRIS (1870–1902), author of *The Octopus* (1901) and *The Pit* (1903), part of an unfinished trilogy, largely conceived, poetic, but violent and crude, on the epic of the wheat; *McTeague* (1899), etc.

     (3) JACK LONDON (1876–1916) combines the harsh detail of the later realist with high-colored romantic themes in *The Call of the Wild* (1903), his most famous and most perfect book, the story of a dog who joins the wolf pack

in the Klondike, *The Sea-Wolf* (1904), *The Game* (1905), and *Before Adam* (907); with zeal for reform in *The Iron Heel* (1908).

(4) THEODORE DREISER (1871–   ), reacting naïvely against the narrowness of his Middle-Western upbringing, represents characters in successful or unsuccessful conflict with conventional standards in *Sister Carrie* (1900), *Jenny Gerhardt* (1911), *The Financier* (1912), *The Titan* (1914), *An American Tragedy* (1925). Once thought startlingly frank, still impressive for their emotional sincerity, these novels are chiefly important for their influence on later naturalistic pessimists and on the enemies of "bourgeois" society. As art they are negligible: bad in structure, shoddy in style, feeble in ideas.

C. Writers of romance
   1. Reaction from realism; promoted by the influence of Stevenson and by the Spanish-American War; materials from history, medieval and Renaissance, but chiefly American—the settlement, the Revolution, the frontier, the Civil War, etc.
   2. Some of the more important romancers were: MARY HARTWELL CATHERWOOD (1847–1902), author of *The Romance of Dollard* (1889), *The Lady of Fort St. John* (1891), *Lazarre* (1901), etc.; S. WEIR MITCHELL (1829–1914), author of *Hugh Wynne, Free Quaker* (1897), perhaps the best novel of its class, *The Adventures of François* (1898), and *The Red City* (1908)—which brought him more fame than his quieter, more realistic stories, *Characteristics* (1892), *Circumstance* (1901), etc.; CHARLES MAJOR (1856–1913), author of *When Knighthood Was in Flower*, (1898); MARY JOHNSTON (1870–1936), author of the vivid, sentimental *Prisoners of Hope* (1898), *To Have and To Hold* (1900), etc.; PAUL LEICESTER FORD* (1865–1902), author of the soundly based but mechanical *Janice Meredith* (1899); WINSTON CHURCHILL* (1871–   ), author of *Richard Carvel* (1899), a charming story of the Revolution; *The Crisis* (1901); *The Crossing* (1904); MAURICE THOMPSON (1844–1901), author of *Alice of Old Vincennes* (1900). *The Slim Princess* (1907) of GEORGE ADE (1866–   ), a parody on the *Prisoner of Zenda* type of romance, marks about the end of the vogue.

3. Conspicuous among the later romancers often distinguished by a skilful use of realism in detail, are: JAMES BRANCH CABELL (1879-   ), fine, adroit, mannered, fantastical to the point of tedium, in *The Cream of the Jest* (1917), *Beyond Life* (1919), etc.; JOSEPH HERGESHEIMER* (1880-   ), whose *Three Black Pennys* (1917), *Java Head* (1919), and *Linda Condon* (1919) add sound characterization to romantic action and atmosphere, but in *Cytherea* (1921), *The Bright Shawl* (1922), etc., exotic melodrama rules.

D. Novelists with a purpose

1. Interest in social, economic, political, moral, and religious questions appears in the works of many novelists, predominating in a large number of them; adds somewhat to the seriousness of the works, but often impairs artistic unity.

2. Pioneers in the field include: ALBION W. TOURGEE (1838-1905) in *A Fool's Errand* (1879) and *Bricks without Straw* (1880), on reconstruction in the South; HELEN HUNT JACKSON (1831-85), champion of the defrauded Indian in the eloquent and passionate California romance *Ramona* (1884); THOMAS BAILEY ALDRICH* (1836-1907) in *The Stillwater Tragedy* (1880) and JOHN HAY* (1838-1905) in *The Bread-Winners* (1883), unsympathetic critics of the labor movement; EDWARD BELLAMY (1850-98), author of a widely read Utopian picture of Boston in 2000 A.D., *Looking Backward* (1888); and PAUL LEICESTER FORD* (1865-1902), who drew hints from the career of Grover Cleveland for his exposure of machine politics in *The Honorable Peter Stirling* (1894).

3. Writers of the present century

   a) MARGARET DELAND* (1857-   ), a serious and strong novelist, writes on modern religious problems in *John Ward, Preacher* (1888), and in later novels—*Philip and His Wife* (1894), *The Awakening of Helena Richie* (1906), *The Iron Woman* (1911), and *The Rising Tide* (1916)—on problems of the relations of the sexes.

   b) ROBERT HERRICK (1868-1938), a satirical realist, attacks dishonesty in business and industry in *The Common Lot* (1904) and *A Life for a Life* (1910); social satire appears in *One Woman's Life* (1913) and *Clark's Field* (1914).

    c) WINSTON CHURCHILL* (1871–   ) deals with various political, industrial, and religious problems, in a somewhat melo-dramatic and imitative fashion, in *Coniston* (1906), *The Inside of the Cup* (1912), *A Far Country* (1915), etc.

    d) UPTON SINCLAIR* (1878–   ) wrote novelized propaganda on the Chicago Stock Yards in *The Jungle* (1906), a coal strike in *King Coal* (1917), newspapers in *The Brass Check* (1919), etc.

    e) WILLIAM ALLEN WHITE (1868–   ), Kansas editor and politi-cal liberal, deals with industrial problems in *A Certain Rich Man* (1909) and *In the Heart of a Fool* (1918); in lighter vein are *The Court of Boyville* (1899) and *The Martial Adventures of Henry and Me* (1918).

    f) BRAND WHITLOCK (1869–1934) wrote without bias of politics in *The Thirteenth District* (1902) and *Big Matt* (1928), of penol-ogy in *The Turn of the Balance* (1907).

    g) HAMLIN GARLAND'S* *Hesper* (1903) dealt with labor trouble at Cripple Creek; and ERNEST POOLE (1880–   ) in the his-torically important but badly written *The Harbor* (1915) de-scribed a young writer converted to revolutionary proletarian-ism by participation in a dockyard strike.

THE SHORT STORY

I. Evolution of the Type

A. Contribution of Poe and Hawthorne—idea of unity of theme and tone; of Hawthorne—central meaning, and analysis of character; of transitional writers—some groping toward realism.

B. Further advance after 1870: (1) perfected handling of the actual; (2) general adoption of the methods of compression and economy exemplified by Poe; (3) development of technical devices—dramatic contrast, cumulative suspense, surprise, and paradox.

C. Short story today a catholic form, ranging from the apologue to the tale or the "novelette"; but the main body of practice em-phasizes unity of theme and tone, swiftness, compression, and climax; individual variations as to realism, character portrayal, surprise, etc.

II. **Francis Bret Harte, "Bret Harte"*** (1836–1902)

   A. Born in New York State; after 1878 in Europe; 1854–71 in California, where in crude life and characters of mining days he found materials for his successful stories and poems. Influence on him of Dickens and French realists; in turn influenced many later American writers and Kipling.

   B. Characteristics of his stories

     1. His first stories, which met with extraordinary success, mark the beginning of the modern short story; combine rapidity, brevity, and unity with Dickens-like sentiment and with the new element of "local color," i.e., a minute representation of local peculiarities of scene, habits, and speech.

     2. The later stories mostly work the same vein; usually longer, and less impressive through loss of intensity; plots become stereotyped and loose, characters mainly indistinct and conventional.

     3. His fame rests on: (1) the impetus he gave to the "local color" movement, (2) the creation of a few memorable types of frontier character—the illiterate miner, the gentleman gambler, the stage-coach driver; a few early stories which are brief, dramatic, touched with a happy blending of humor and pathos, and preserve a vivid if exaggerated picture of a dramatic moment in the development of the Far West.

   C. Among his many stories may be mentioned: "The Luck of Roaring Camp," "Tennessee's Partner," and "The Outcasts of Poker Flat" (in *The Luck of Roaring Camp and Other Stories*, 1870); "How Santa Claus Came to Simpson's Bar" and "The Iliad of Sandy Bar" (in *Mrs. Skagg's Husbands and Other Sketches*, 1873); *Flip A California Romance* (1882); *In the Carquinez Woods* (1883) *The Argonauts of North Liberty* (1888); "The Bell-Ringer of Angel's" (1893); *In a Hollow of the Hills* (1895).

III. **Later Workers in Local Color**

   A. New England life is depicted intimately by SARAH ORNE JEWETT* (1849–1909), who wrote stories of admirable finish and serenity, including "Miss Tempy's Watchers," "The Dulham Ladies," "A White Heron" (1886), and *A Native of Wimby* (1893); MARY E.

WILKINS FREEMAN* (1862–1930), most poignant and concentrated, but concerned chiefly with the somber barrenness, defeat, and repression of New England rural decadence, in the stories of *A Humble Romance and Other Stories* (1887) and *A New England Nun and Other Stories* (1891), notably the two title stories and "Life-Everlasting," "Louisa," "A Gala Dress," "A Village Singer," "The Revolt of Mother," "A Village Lear," etc.; ALICE BROWN (1857–   ), author of *Meadow Grass* (1895), *Tiverton Tales* (1899), etc., as well as novels and a prize play, *Children of Earth* (1915).

B. The Middle States
   1. New York City figures in the stories, such as *Gallegher and Other Stories* (1891) and *Van Bibber and Others* (1892), of RICHARD HARDING DAVIS (1864–1916); also in those of H. C. BUNNER,* EDITH WHARTON,* "O. HENRY,"* and others whose chief emphasis is not on the local scene.
   2. A Pennsylvania village is the chief scene of *Old Chester Tales* (1898) and *Dr. Lavendar's People* (1903), by MARGARET DELAND* (1857–   ).

C. The Middle and the Far West: EUGENE MANLOVE RHODES (1869–1935), author of romantic tales of the Southwest, as *Good Men and True* (1911) and *Bransford in Arcadia* (1914); THOMAS A. JANVIER (1849–1913), author of the Southwestern dialect stories, *Santa-Fe's Partner* (1907), who presents a more exotic romance with finish of style in *Stories of Old New Spain* (1891), *From the South of France* (1912), and *At the Casa Napoléon* (1914), as well as in his longer stories, *The Aztec Treasure House* (1890) and *In the Sargasso Sea* (1898); ALICE FRENCH, "Octave Thanet" (1850–1934), who portrays life in Iowa and Arkansas in *Knitters in the Sun* (1887), etc., HAMLIN GARLAND* (1860–1940), bitter realist in *Main-Travelled Roads* (1891), etc.; SHERWOOD ANDERSON* (1876–   ), whose extreme realism, or naturalism, distorts reality in the powerful sketches in *Winesburg, Ohio* (1919) and *The Triumph of the Egg* (1921).

D. The South: RICHARD M. JOHNSTON (1822–98) was a pioneer in his truthful but slight *Georgia Sketches* (1864) and *Dukesborough Tales* (1871); the romance and tragedy of Louisiana life are presented in GEORGE W. CABLE's* "'Sieur George" (1873), as well as the other stories of *Old Creole Days* (1879) and *Madame Delphine* (1881), in *Monsieur Motte* (1888) and *Balcony Stories* (1893) by GRACE E. KING (1851–1932), and in *Bayou Folk* (1894) by KATE CHOPIN (1851–1904); THOMAS NELSON PAGE* preserves the romance of Virginia in *In Ole Virginia* (1887); CONSTANCE FENIMORE WOOLSON* (1848–94) shows delicacy and truthful realism in *Rodman the Keeper* (1880); MARY N. MURFREE, "Charles Egbert Craddock" (1850–1922) is picturesque but melodramatic in *In the Tennessee Mountains* (1884); Kentucky is depicted by JAMES LANE ALLEN* (1849–1925) in *Flute and Violin* (1891), *The Kentucky Cardinal* (1894), etc., and by JOHN FOX, JR.,* (1863–1919) in *A Cumberland Vendetta and Other Stories* (1896); JOEL CHANDLER HARRIS (1848–1908) preserved valuable animal folklore and surpassed all others in depiction of negro character, in *Uncle Remus, his Songs and his Sayings* (1880), *Nights with Uncle Remus* (1883), and *Uncle Remus and his Friends* (1892); and ALBERT BIGELOW PAINE (1861–1937), though himself a New Englander, in his *Hollow Tree* stories (3 series, 1901, 1910, 1916) tells for children—and adults—with admirable dry humor the adventures of "the Coon, the Possum, and the Old Black Crow," assigning them human personalities and a background which suggests the vicinity of Mason and Dixon's Line.

IV. Later Contributors to the Technical Development of the Short Story

A. THOMAS BAILEY ALDRICH* (1836–1907) in "Marjorie Daw" (1873) wrote the first genuinely successful short story with a surprise in the last sentence; otherwise a commonplace tale.

B. FRANK R. STOCKTON* (1834–1902)

1. Developed to a kind of perfection the whimsical or fantastic tale for children, giving it a literary charm and an inner meaning which carry an appeal to the adult, in such stories as *The Floating Prince and Other Fairy Tales* (1881), and "The Griffin and the Minor Canon," "The Bee-Man of Orn," and "Old Pipes and the Dryad" (in *The Bee-Man of Orn and Other Fanciful Tales*, 1887).

2. His most famous story, "The Lady or the Tiger?" (1882), with its surprise ending created a widespread sensation; other characteristic stories are "The Transferred Ghost" (in *The Lady or the Tiger? and Other Stories*, 1884), "The Christmas Wreck," "A Tale

of Negative Gravity," and "The Remarkable Wreck of the Thomas Hyke" (in *The Christmas Wreck and Other Stories*, 1886), and "The Widow's Cruise" (in *A Story-Teller's Pack*, 1897).

C. HENRY CUYLER BUNNER* (1855–96) wrote with a French finish and grace stories in which humor and sentiment are delicately blended, as *Short Sixes; Stories to Be Read While the Candle Burns* (1891), *Zadoc Pine and Other Stories* (1891), *More Short Sixes* (1894), and *Love in Old Cloathes and Other Stories* (1896).

D. AMBROSE BIERCE (1842–1913) wrought like Poe artistically subtle. intellectual, but unreal and ghastly tales, as those in *In the Midst of Life* (originally published as *Tales of Soldiers and Civilians*, 1891).

E. STEPHEN CRANE* (1871–1900) anticipated the brutal realism of the naturalistic writers of today, but without their pruriency; his aim always to tell the literal truth and to keep down his style to the literal level. His vividness, power, and harshness, occasionally mitigated with humor or poetic touches, appear in "The Open Boat" (1898), story of an actual shipwreck, "The Monster" and "The Blue Hotel" (in *The Monster and Other Stories*, 1899) and in the collection *Wounds in the Rain* (1900), stories of the Spanish-American War; the harshness is absent from the stories of *enfants terribles*, *Whilomville Stories* (1900).

F. WILLIAM SYDNEY PORTER, "O. Henry" (1862–1910), carried to the highest point technical dexterity in the manipulation of short story materials and devices in a long series of extremely popular stories, largely of the "four million" of New York City, begun in 1899 Adroitness in situation, constant use of suspense, surprise, humor satire, seriousness which turns to mockery, allusiveness, great sensitiveness to the values of style for atmosphere, are generally accompanied by lack of serious intent. The general tone is of superficial smartness or cynicism, except for a few sincerely grim pieces like "The Furnished Room" (in *The Four Million*, 1908). Other characteristic stories are "While the Auto Waits" (in *The Voice of the City*, 1908), "The Hiding of Black Bill" (in *Options*, 1909), and "A Matter of Mean Elevation" and "The Roads We Take" (in *Whirligigs*, 1910).

V. Individual Lines

Individual lines, akin to those of their novels, were followed in the short stories of

A. HENRY JAMES* (1843–1916)

1. Early stories mostly crude, partly imitative of Hawthorne, of which "The Passionate Pilgrim" (1871) is the best known.
2. Mature work, in longish stories wrought with his characteristic analytical detail and shadowy implications, dealing with (a) the artistic life, as "The Author of Beltraffio" (1885), "The Aspern Papers" (1888); (b) simple themes made dramatic and strange by presenting them in a twilight of innuendo, as in "The Private Life" (1893) and "The Visits" (1893); (c) the horrible, as in "The Turn of the Screw" (1898).

B. EDITH WHARTON* (1862–1937)

1. Studies of tragic passion, as "The Duchess at Prayer" (in *Crucial Instances*, 1901).
2. Studies of the artistic life, as "The Verdict" and "The Pot Boiler" (in *The Hermit and the Wild Woman*, 1908), "The Daunt Diana" (in *Tales of Men and Ghosts*, 1910).
3. Studies of crises and conflicts in a cosmopolitan society, as "The Last Asset" (in *The Hermit and the Wild Woman*, 1908) and "The Long Run" (in *Xingu and Other Stories*, 1916).
4. Experiments with the supernatural, as "The Lady's Maid's Bell" (in *The Descent of Man and Other Stories*, 1904), "The Eyes" and "Afterward" (in *Tales of Men and Ghosts*, 1910) and "The Triumph of Night" (in *Xingu and Other Stories*, 1916).

POETRY

I. General Characteristics

Many minor poets from all parts of the country, but few of real distinction; much energy and much versatility of form. The period divides conveniently at 1900.

II. The Earlier Poets (1870–1900)

A. The East and the South.   Writers mostly follow traditional fashions, with considerable felicity but slender inspiration.

1. Poets distinctly of the "classical" tradition
   a) LUCY LARCOM (1826–93) and CELIA THAXTER (1836–94), who wrote of nature and the sea, and the sisters ALICE CARY (1820–71) and PHOEBE CARY (1824–71) echo the moods of Longfellow and Whittier.
   b) HELEN HUNT JACKSON* (1831–85) wrote finished poems of intimate personal emotion, as "Spinning" (1874).
   c) THOMAS BAILEY ALDRICH* (1836–1907) in earlier volumes, as *Baby Bell and Other Poems* (1856), given to cloying sensuousness, gains in intensity and restraint while retaining exquisite finish in his later poems, as in the volumes *Windham Towers* (1889), *The Sisters' Tragedy with Other Poems* (1891), and his personally selected volume, *Songs and Sonnets* (1906).
   d) EDMUND CLARENCE STEDMAN* (1833–1908) is remembered for the Civil War poem, "How Old Brown Took Harper's Ferry" (1859), and the finely wrought "Pan in Wall Street" (1867).
   e) RICHARD WATSON GILDER (1844–1909), editor of the *Century Magazine*, wrote melodiously, often of music and the other arts; poets of kindred gifts are HENRY VAN DYKE* (1852–1933) and GEORGE E. WOODBERRY* (1855–1930).
   f) JOHN B. TABB (1845–1909), HENRY CUYLER BUNNER* (1855–96), and CLINTON SCOLLARD (1860–1932) possess exquisite grace and ease.
   g) EDWARD ROWLAND SILL (1841–87), close to the New England tradition though long resident in the West, wrote poems of brooding religious doubt, as "The Fool's Prayer" and "Opportunity."
   h) MADISON CAWEIN (1865–1914) was a copious and rich but diffuse Southern poet.
2. More distinctive poets
   a) SIDNEY LANIER (1842–81)
      (1) Native of Georgia, soldier in the Confederate Army, musician, lecturer at Johns Hopkins.
      (2) Poems sometimes vague and marred by studied conceits, but full of subtle music—in part secured by a novel freedom of rhythm—and marked by intense feeling, especially for nature and against injustice, and by originality of phrase.

(3) Among his poems are: (a) nature poems—"The Mocking Bird" (1877), "The Marshes of Glynn" (1879), and "Sunrise" (1882); (b) other striking long poems—"Corn" (1875), "The Symphony" (1875), the terrible "Revenge of Hamish" (1878), the eloquent, patriotic "Psalm of the West" (1876), and the vivid, pathetic "How Love Looked for Hell" (1884); (c) pregnant short poems—"Evening Song" (1877), "The Stirrup-Cup" (1877), and "A Ballad of Trees and the Master" (1880).

b) EMILY DICKINSON (1830–86), a cloistered Massachusetts poet, phrased odd and whimsical meditations on life in brief poems of startling and naïve originality, vivid, pungent, subtle, and imaginative; as "This Is My Letter," "I Died for Beauty," "I Never Saw a Moor," "In the Garden," "Simplicity," "Forbidden Fruit," "To Make a Prairie." She was akin to the seventeenth-century metaphysical poets and anticipated the break with traditional moods and imagery in the poetry of today.

c) RICHARD HOVEY (1864–1900), collaborator with BLISS CARMAN (1861–1929) in Songs from Vagabondia (3 series, 1894, 1896, 1900), looks forward to the abandon of the new century in the lyrical fervor of his delight in vagabondage and Bohemian fellowship.

d) STEPHEN CRANE* (1871–1900), in brief, strikingly vivid, but crude poems, The Black Riders and Other Lines (1895) and War is Kind (1899), anticipates the mood of the "new" poetry by his rebellious attack on conventional religion in rebelliously "free" verse.

B. Western poets, 1870–1900
  1. Like Whitman, inclined to turn from traditional subjects to "life"; to be vigorous and vital, but unfinished, crude, or cheap. Reflected the ideals of a newer society; seemed to Europe peculiarly American.
  2. Poets of the frontier
    a) BRET HARTE* (1836–1902) in the vernacular poems of life in the mining camps, "Plain Language from Truthful James," "The Society upon the Stanislaus," "Chiquita," "Dow's

Flat," "In the Tunnel," etc. (collected in *East and West Poems*, 1871), and JOHN HAY* (1838–1905), in *Pike County Ballads* (1871), popularized the crude Western character, "the Pike," and prepared the way for a flood of dialect poems.

b) CINCINNATUS H. MILLER, "Joaquin Miller" (1841–1913), called the "Oregon Byron," in copious, diffuse, declamatory, high-colored poems somewhat in the mood of Whitman, gives the most adequate picture of the stirring life and the grand scenery of the Far West. Published *Songs of the Sierras* (London, 1870), *Songs of the Desert* (1875), etc.; typical poems are: "The Last Taschastas," "Kit Carson's Ride," "Crossing the Plains." "Exodus for Oregon," "Westward Ho!," "The Ship in the Desert," "The Yosemite Valley," and "Columbus."

3. Poets of homely life, chiefly in the Middle West

a) JOHN JAMES PIATT (1835–1917) and his wife SARAH MORGAN PIATT (1836–1912) wrote simply, in conventional forms, of rural life.

b) WILL CARLETON (1845–1912) won widespread success with his homely, sentimental poems, mainly in dialect, including *Farm Ballads* (1873), *Farm Legends* (1875), *City Ballads* (1885), etc., of which the most famous are "Out of the Old House, Nancy," "Betsy and I Are Out," and "Over the Hills to the Poor House."

c) JAMES WHITCOMB RILEY (1849–1916) in his many Hoosier dialect poems, beginning with *The Old Swimmin' Hole and 'Leven More Poems* (1883) and including the popular "An Old Sweetheart of Mine" and "When the Frost Is on the Punkin," addressed effectively the heart of the average man; influenced later poets, such as SAM WALTER FOSS (1858–1911), of Massachusetts, author of *Back Country Poems* (1894), etc.

4. EUGENE FIELD (1850–95) makes happy use of humor and sentiment in *A Little Book of Western Verse* (1890), *Love-Songs of Childhood* (1894), and the adroit variations upon Horatian themes in *Echoes from the Sabine Farm* (1893).

5. WILLIAM VAUGHN MOODY* (1869–1910), scholarly and sensitive poet, using traditional forms under influence of Rossetti and

Browning; combined religious and political idealism with the freely inquiring scientific spirit of the modern world, in poems full of power and beauty, though sometimes chaotic in general effect. Besides a prose play, *The Great Divide* (1906), and an ambitious uncompleted trilogy of poetic dramas in blank verse dealing grandly but somewhat indistinctly with the problem of evil and the relation of God and man (*The Fire-Bringer*, 1904; *The Masque of Judgment*, 1900; and "I Am the Woman" and "The Death of Eve," 1901, preliminary studies for the third drama), he wrote stirring patriotic poems, as "On a Soldier Fallen in the Philippines" and the splendid "anti-imperialistic" ode "An Ode in Time of Hesitation" (1900), and shorter poems largely concerned with problems of modern thought, as "Gloucester Moors," "The Brute," and "The Menagerie."

III. The Later Poets (1900–1920)

A. Chief tendency to experimentation and license with respect to (1) metrical forms, (2) decorum of speech, (3) ideas or ideals. The poems have sincerity, vigor, and incisiveness, but often suffer from excessive subjectivity and lack of perspective. The break with the last century brought freedom from outworn formulas but some loss of the rich and stabilizing force of tradition.

B. Conservatives—in form and partly in substance

　1. EDWIN ARLINGTON ROBINSON (1869–1935) writes with intellectuality, finish, and warmth in *The Children of the Night* (1896), *Captain Craig* (1902), *The Town down the River* (1910), *The Man against the Sky* (1916). Psychological insight and dramatic power distinguish his Arthurian trilogy, *Merlin* (1917), *Lancelot* (1920), and *Tristram* (1927), and the more colloquial modern tales, *Roman Bartholow* (1923), *Talifer* (1933), etc.

　2. JOSEPHINE PRESTON PEABODY MARKS* (1874–1922) writes with rich melody and some dramatic force in *The Wayfarers* (1898), *The Singing Leaves* (1903), *The Singing Man* (1911), and *Harvest Moon* (1916).

　3. NICHOLAS VACHEL LINDSAY (1879–1931) writes lyrics of a conspicuous singing quality, in his volumes, *General William Booth Enters into Heaven and Other Poems* (1913), *The Congo and Other*

Poems (1914), and *The Chinese Nightingale and Other Poems* (1917).

4. SARA TEASDALE (1884–1933) has sharpness of imagery, epigrammatic terseness, and exquisite finish of form in *Rivers to the Sea.* (1915), *Love Songs* (1917), and *Flame and Shadow* (1920).

5. CONRAD AIKEN (1889–　　), influenced successively by Masefield, Masters, and Eliot, attains lyrical beauty but suffers from Freudian obsessions in *The Jig of Forslin* (1916), etc.

6. ALAN SEEGER (1888–1916) before his death in battle had written a few moving poems inspired by the Great War, including "I Have a Rendezvous with Death" and "Ode in Memory of the American Volunteers Fallen for France."

C. Radicals

1. EDGAR LEE MASTERS (1869–　　) created a great sensation by his *Spoon River Anthology* (1914–15), brutally frank and mostly depressing epitaphs exposing with savage satire the pettiness and vice of the inhabitants of a Mid-Western village—written in a rough, unrhymed verse; in similar vein are *Songs and Satires* (1916), *The Great Valley* (1916), and *Toward the Gulf* (1918).

2. The "Imagists"

   a) A group of poets who demanded freedom in choice of subjects, and aimed at sharp images, and new and freer rhythms as against those of "regular verse." Sometimes successful, often they attain only the rhythm of prose, and by concentration on "images" at the expense of ideas produce an effect of thinness and narrowness.

   b) Among the more important are: AMY LOWELL (1874–1925), author of *A Dome of Many-coloured Glass* (1912), *Sword Blades and Poppy Seed* (1914), etc., who has vividness and some delicacy; EZRA POUND (1885–　　), author of *Personæ* (1909), *Ripostes* (1912), *Cantos* (1930 ff.), etc.; JOHN GOULD FLETCHER (1886–　　), author of *Goblins and Pagodas* (1916), etc.; T. S. ELIOT* (1888–　　), author of *Prufrock* (London, 1917), *Poems* (1920), and *The Waste Land* (1922).

3. CARL SANDBURG (1878–　　) has united beauty and violence in *Chicago Poems* (1916), *Corn Huskers* (1918), *Smoke and Steel* (1920), and *Slabs of the Sunburnt West* (1922).

THE DRAMA

I. Theatrical Conditions

In the sixties and seventies stock companies still flourished, acting dramas largely imitations of foreign works, melodramatic or sentimental in character. In the eighties modern conditions began to develop with the coming of great managers, under whom the drama suffered the handicaps of (1) the "star" system, (2) frank commercialization; the plays began profitably to emphasize external realism, but sacrificed ideas. After 1870 an increasing number of serious, skilful writers.

II. Leading Professional Dramatists

A. BRONSON HOWARD (1842–1908), first important modern dramatist, worked with conscientious care and promoted the use of American themes, in his plays of contemporary manners, *Saratoga* (1870[1]), *Young Mrs. Winthrop* (1882), *The Henrietta* (1887), *Shenandoah* (1889), etc.

B. JAMES A. HERNE (1839–1901), who added playwriting to acting, beginning with *Hearts of Oak* (1879), went farther than Howard in realistic portrayal of humble American life, as in *Shore Acres* (1892) and *Sag Harbor* (1900); in *Margaret Fleming* (1890) wrote "the first psychological drama."

C. AUGUSTUS THOMAS (1857–1934) expert technician, serious, and independent, dealt with local conditions in *Alabama* (1891), *Mizzoura* (1893), and *Arizona* (1899), wrote brilliant dialogue in *The Other Girl* (1903) and *Mrs. Leffingwell's Boots* (1905), and turned to psychic phenomena and other modern themes in *The Witching Hour* (1907), probably his greatest play, in *The Harvest Moon* (1909), and in *As a Man Thinks* (1911).

D. DAVID BELASCO (1859–1931), successful in the struggle for an independent theater, unusually skilful in scenic and lighting effects and in adapting plays to "stars," is best known for his high-colored, romantic *Madame Butterfly* (1900), *The Darling of the Gods* (1902) and *The Girl of the Golden West* (1905).

E. WILLIAM GILLETTE (1855–1937) shows great technical skill both in farce, as in *Too Much Johnson* (1894) and *Because She Loved Him So*

[1] Unless otherwise noted, the dates given with plays are of their first acting.

(1899), and in melodramatic pieces such as *Held by the Enemy* (1886) and *Secret Service* (1896), Civil War plays, and *Sherlock Holmes* (1899).

F. CLYDE FITCH (1865–1909) wrote many extremely clever plays of some literary quality, but usually marked by shallowness and smartness rather than thorough grasp of character; somewhat too many written for "stars." Among his best plays are *The Climbers* (1901), social satire, *The Girl with the Green Eyes* (1902) and *The Truth* (1906), psychological studies of jealousy and deception, and the powerful *The City* (1909).

G. LANGDON E. MITCHELL (1862–1935) in *The New York Idea* (1906) wrote an excellent satire on divorce, with much of the sparkle of eighteenth-century comedy; also author of successful dramatizations of *Vanity Fair* (1899) and *Pendennis* (1916).

H. Others include: EDWARD B. SHELDON* (1886–   ), clever but rather superficial realist, author of *Salvation Nell* (1908), *The Nigger* (1909), etc.; EUGENE WALTER (1874–   ), author of *Paid in Full* (1908) and *The Easiest Way* (1909); ALBERT E. THOMAS (1872–   ), author of witty social comedies, *Her Husband's Wife* (1910), *The Rainbow* (1912), *Here Are Ladies* (1934), etc.; RACHEL CROTHERS (1878–   ), skilful analyst of women's problems in *The Three of Us* (1906), *A Man's World* (1909), *He and She* (1911), and *Ourselves* (1913), and of current topics in *Nice People* (1920), *Expressing Willie* (1924), *As Husbands Go* (1931), etc.

III. Writers Whose Reputation Is Chiefly Literary

A. Before 1900
1. WILLIAM DEAN HOWELLS* (1837–1920) wrote several comedies, including *A Counterfeit Presentment* (1877[1]) and *A Previous Engagement* (1897), and more than a dozen farces, including *The Parlor Car* (1876), *The Sleeping Car* (1883), and *The Register* (1884), witty and lightly satirical sketches, some successfully produced; early examples of the one-act play.
2. HENRY JAMES* (1843–1916) toiled long at playwriting during 1890–95, but with little success; his *Guy Domville* was acted in 1895.

[1] For the plays of Howells the dates of publication are given.

3. THOMAS BAILEY ALDRICH* (1836–1907) wrote the poetic drama, *Judith of Bethulia* (acted 1904).

C. Later Writers

1. WILLIAM VAUGHN MOODY* (1869–1910) made an unexpected success with his powerful prose drama, *The Great Divide* (1906; acted 1906), with its grasp of reality and its passion; *The Faith Healer* (1909; acted 1910) was not a success, though noble and poetic in conception.

2. JOSEPHINE PRESTON PEABODY MARKS* (1874–1922) shows command of atmosphere and character, with poetic grace and some dramatic skill in *Marlowe* (1901), *The Piper* (1909; acted 1910), and *The Wolf of Gubbio* (1913).

3. PERCY MACKAYE (1875–   ), serious, scholarly, poetical, early in touch with the stage as the son of the playwright, STEELE MAC-KAYE (1844–94), has written a wide variety of plays and masques of pretty uniform literary quality, often highly poetical and showing genuine dramatic sense, but for the most part academic and lacking in popular appeal. They include: (*a*) intense poetical dramas—*Fenris the Wolf* (1905), *Jeanne d'Arc* (1906), *Sappho and Phaon* (1907), and the Chinese romance, *A Thousand Years Ago* (1914; acted 1913); (*b*) comedy and satire—*Mater* (1908) on politics; *The Scarecrow* (1908; acted 1909), a pathetic fantasy based on Hawthorne's *Feathertop;* and *Anti-Matrimony* (1910); (*c*) masques and pageants—*The Canterbury Pilgrims* (1903; acted 1909), based on Chaucer's "Prologue"; *Sanctuary, a Bird Masque* (1913), *St. Louis, a Civic Masque* (1914), and *Caliban, a Community Masque* (1916).

IV. The "Little Theater" Movement

A. Dissatisfaction with the commercial theater and drama found expression in the "new theater" venture in New York (1909–12); drama groups sprang up all over the country, with amateur playwrights and amateur or semi-professional players. Much experimenting in lighting and other effects, and in dramatic forms, particularly in the use of short or one-act plays.

B. Aimed to secure a drama (*a*) thoughtful, (*b*) genuinely artistic, (*c*) of literary quality, (*d*) free of hampering stage traditions.

C. Among the more important writers of one-act plays are GEORGE MIDDLETON (1880–   ), author of *Tradition* (1913), *A Good Woman* (1916), etc.; SUSAN GLASPELL* (1882–   ), author of *Trifles* (published 1916) and (with GEORGE C. COOK) of *Suppressed Desires* (published 1916); PERCIVAL WILDE (1887–   ), author of *Catesby* (1922), etc.; and EUGENE G. O'NEILL* (1888–   ), who began as playwright with *Bound East for Cardiff* (1916) and introduced the same rough sailors in later plays, *The Long Voyage Home* (1917), *In the Zone* (1917), and *The Moon of the Caribbees* (1918); *Ile* (1917), story of a whaling captain's dogged search for oil, is perhaps the best.

ESSAYS AND MISCELLANEOUS PROSE

I. Descriptive Essays, Travels, and Autobiographical Sketches

A. CHARLES DUDLEY WARNER* (1829–1900) wrote many popular essays and sketches of Irving-like cultivated ease and quiet, rather old-fashioned humor, in *My Summer in a Garden* (1870), *Backlog Studies* (1872), *My Winter on the Nile* (1876), *Being a Boy* (1877), etc.

B. THOMAS W. HIGGINSON (1823–1911), a minor author in many fields and intimate friend of the great New England group of the mid-century, recorded the memories of a lifetime in his genial *Cheerful Yesterdays* (1898).

C. JOHN HAY* (1838–1905) in *Castilian Days* (1871); WILLIAM DEAN HOWELLS* (1837–1920) in *Venetian Life* (1866), *London Films* (1905), *Certain Delightful English Towns* (1906), and *Familiar Spanish Travels* (1913); HENRY JAMES* (1843–1916) in *Transatlantic Sketches* (1875), *A Little Tour in France* (1884), *Portraits of Places* (1884), and *The American Scene* (1907); and EDITH WHARTON* (1862–1937) in *Italian Backgrounds* (1905), *A Motor Flight Through France* (1908), and *Fighting France* (1915)—all continue with a latter-day exquisiteness of finish the long series of impressions which began with Irving.

D. WILLIAM DEAN HOWELLS* in *My Literary Passions* (1895), *Impressions and Experiences* (1896), *Literary Friends and Acquaintance* (1900), and *The Years of My Youth* (1916) and HENRY JAMES* in *A Small Boy and Others* (1913), *Notes of a Son and Brother* (1913), and *The Middle Years* (1917) combine valuable autobiography with literary comment and criticism.

II. Familiar Essays

A. AGNES REPPLIER (1858–   ) has wit, classical polish, and shrewd criticism of books and life in her *Books and Men* (1888), *Essays in Idleness* (1893), *Compromises* (1904), *Americans and Others* (1912), etc.

B. SAMUEL McCHORD CROTHERS (1857–1927) presents a wise and kindly philosophy suffused with a whimsical humor in *The Gentle Reader* (1903), *The Pardoner's Wallet* (1905), *By the Christmas Fire* (1908), and *Humanly Speaking* (1912).

C. EDWARD S. MARTIN (1856–1939), successor of Mr. Howells in "The Easy Chair" of *Harper's Magazine*, author of *Lucid Intervals* (1900), *The Luxury of Children, and Other Luxuries* (1904), *Reflections of a Beginning Husband* (1913), etc.

D. FINLEY PETER DUNNE (1867–1936) handled questions of the day with pungent humor and shrewdness in the Irish monologues of *Mr. Dooley in Peace and in War* (1898), *Mr. Dooley in the Hearts of His Countrymen* (1899), *Mr. Dooley's Philosophy* (1900), etc.

III. Critical Essays

A. Many books containing the critical opinions and judgments of men of letters, and an increasing body of sound technical work by scholars, but still little distinguished writing by professional literary critics.

B. Writers who divide their interest between criticism and other fields: EDMUND C. STEDMAN* (1833–1908), author of the discriminating *Victorian Poets* (1875), *Poets of America* (1885), etc.; WILLIAM DEAN HOWELLS,* who defended the cause of realism and set forth his literary tastes in *Criticism and Fiction* (1892), *My Literary Passions* (1895), etc.; HENRY JAMES,* who wrote with great penetration in *Hawthorne* (1879), *Partial Portraits* (1888), *Essays in London and Elsewhere* (1893), etc.; SIDNEY LANIER* (1842–81), whose acute and suggestive *Science of English Verse* (1880), *The English Novel* (1883), *Shakspere and his Forerunners* (1902), etc., show the defect of a limited scholarly equipment; GEORGE E. WOODBERRY* (1855–1930), author of *Edgar Allan Poe* (1885), *Studies in Letters and Life* (1890), *Nathaniel Hawthorne* (1902), etc.

C. More formal critics: BRANDER MATTHEWS (1852–1939), who combines learning and taste with readableness in *French Dramatists of the Nineteenth Century* (1881, 1891), *Shakespeare as a Playwright* (1913), etc.; BARRETT WENDELL (1855–1921), New Englander and cosmopolitan, author of *A Literary History of America* (1900), *The Temper of the Seventeenth Century in English Literature* (1904), etc.; BLISS PERRY (1860–   ), urbane and of wide culture in *A Study of Prose Fiction* (1902), *Walt Whitman, his Life and Work* (1906), *Park-Street Papers* (1909), *Carlyle* (1915), etc.; IRVING BABBITT (1865–1933), trenchant and vehement defender of the classical conception of art in *A New Laokoon* (1910), *The Masters of Modern French Criticism* (1912), and *Rousseau and Romanticism* (1919); WILLIAM C. BROWNELL (1851–1928), independent and intellectual but over-subtle and condescending, in *French Traits* (1889), *Victorian Prose Masters* (1901), and *American Prose Masters* (1909); WILLIAM WINTER (1836–1917), foremost American dramatic critic, author of *Henry Irving* (1885), *Shadows of the Stage* (1892–93), *The Life and Art of Edwin Booth* (1894), *Shakespeare on the Stage* (2 series, 1911, 1915), etc., PAUL ELMER MORE (1864–1937), the greatest conservative critic, distinguished for breadth and soundness of learning, solidity, and a clear-cut critical point of view; author of *Shelburne Essays* (14 series, 1904–36); HENRY L. MENCKEN (1880–   ), independent and stimulating, author of *Prejudices* (3 series, 1919–22), *The American Language* (1919, 1921); STUART P. SHERMAN (1881–1926), acute and pungent critic, of catholic and discriminating taste, author of *On Contemporary Literature* (1917), *Americans* (1922), *The Genius of America* (1923).

D. Interpretation and re-creation, rather than formal exposition and criticism, appear in delightful form in *Roads from Rome* (1913) by ANNE C. E. ALLINSON (1871–1932), author, with FRANCIS G. ALLINSON, of *Greek Lands and Letters* (1909).

IV. Nature Essayists

A. JOHN BURROUGHS (1837–1921), akin to Thoreau, influenced by Whitman, foremost in his field, wrote simply and with full knowledge in *Wake Robin* (1871), *Winter Sunshine* (1875), *Birds and Poets* (1877), *Locusts and Wild Honey* (1879), *Riverby* (1894), etc.

B. JOHN MUIR (1838–1914) wrote with eloquent poetic feeling of the wilder Western scenes, as in *The Mountains of California* (1894), *Our National Parks* (1901), *My First Summer in the Sierras* (1911), etc.

C. Minor nature writers include: HARRIET MANN MILLER, "Olive Thorne Miller" (1831–1918), author of *Little Folks in Feather and Fur* (1879), etc.; WILLIAM HAMILTON GIBSON (1850–96), author of *Camp Life in the Woods* (1876), *Sharp Eyes* (1891), etc.; HENRY VAN DYKE* (1852–1933), author of *Little Rivers* (1895) and *Fisherman's Luck* (1899); DALLAS LORE SHARP (1870–1929), author of *The Lay of the Land* (1908), *The Face of the Fields* (1911), etc.; STEWART EDWARD WHITE (1873–   ), author of *The Silent Places* (1904), and stories of the out of doors, as *The Blazed Trail* (1902); WALTER PRICHARD EATON (1878–   ), author of *Green Trails and Upland Pastures* (1917), *In Berkshire Fields* (1919), *On the Edge of the Wilderness* (1920).

V. Other Prose Writers

A. History, biography, and government

1. ULYSSES S. GRANT (1822–85) told an absorbing story with effective simplicity in his *Personal Memoirs* (2 vols., 1885, 1886).

2. JOHN FISKE* (1842–1901) wrote a long series of histories of the United States, picturesque and graphic as narrative but unfortunately inaccurate, including *The Discovery of America* (1892), *The American Revolution* (1891), etc.

3. WOODROW WILSON (1856–1924) revealed his great powers of analysis and synthesis and a firm, incisive style in his political and literary works, *The State* (1889), *An Old Master and Other Political Essays* (1893), and *Mere Literature and Other Essays* (1896); his *History of the American People* (5 vols., 1902) has a similar grasp of materials and a vivid style; his state papers and wartime addresses prepared during his terms as president give him secure place among great political leaders for their happy combination of simplicity and elevation, deep feeling, idealistic vision, and practical sagacity.

4. Others include: HENRY C. LEA (1825–1909), author of *A History of the Inquisition* (3 vols., 1888), etc.; ANDREW D. WHITE

1832–1918), college administrator and diplomat, author of *The Warfare of Science with Theology* (2 vols., 1896); JOHN G. NICOLAY (1832–1901) and JOHN HAY* (1838–1905), authors of *Abraham Lincoln, A History* (10 vols., 1890), ALFRED T. MAHAN (1840–1914), author of the internationally famous *The Influence of Sea Power upon History* (1890); THEODORE ROOSEVELT (1858–1919), author of many works in a simple, vigorous, sometimes picturesque style, including *The History of the Naval War of 1812* (1882), *The Winning of the West* (1889–96), etc.

B. Science and philosophy: Writers include: JOHN FISKE* (1842–1901), who expounded the doctrine of evolution in *The Unseen World* (1876), *Darwinism and Other Essays* (1879), *The Idea of God* (1883), etc.; JOSIAH ROYCE (1855–1917), author of *The Religious Aspect of Philosophy* (1885), *The World and the Individual* (1900–1901), *The Philosophy of Loyalty* (1908), etc.; WILLIAM JAMES (1842–1910), who wrote with charming simplicity *The Will to Believe and Other Essays in Popular Philosophy* (1897), *The Varieties of Religious Experience* (1902), *Pragmatism* (1907).

C. Oratory

1. HENRY W. GRADY (1851–89), of Georgia, in his addresses combined much of old-fashioned emotional appeal with modern idealism, as in *The New South* (1886).

2. BOOKER T. WASHINGTON (1859?–1915), born in slavery, became the leader of his race by virtue of his famous address at the opening of the Atlanta Exposition in 1895; author also of the autobiography, *Up from Slavery* (1901).

LITERATURE BETWEEN WARS

GENERAL TENDENCIES

I. Changes in American Life

The tendencies observed in the period preceding the World War (cf. p. 57) have become more pronounced in the "boom decade" (1919–29) and the "depression decade" (1929–39). Particularly notable are:

A. The complex reactions in American thinking to political developments abroad: hope for world-peace (gradually waning), an intensified nationalism, the establishment of totalitarian states, the weakening of democracies, and the conquest of weak nations.

B. The struggle, intense and indecisive, over projects for economic and social reform.

II. Currents in American Literature

Here, too, former tendencies (cf. pp. 57–58) have continued and gained in strength.

FICTION SINCE THE WORLD WAR

I. Principal Developments

A. The rapid extension of the naturalistic movement. "Naturalism is pessimistic realism, with a philosophy that sets man in a mechanical world . . . ." (Parrington, III, 325). It is objective; it accepts the behaviorist psychology (often with a Freudian emphasis), hence seeing man's acts as animal reflexes determined by heredity and environment. It tends to be amorphous in structure, combining "stream of consciousness" and "slice of life"; it is bare and unintellectual in style, brutal and "sexy" in materials.

B. The rise and decline of proletarianism. Accepting naturalism's criticism of man in present society, the proletarian novel repudiates pessimism for an optimistic, "romantic" Marxianism.

C. A partial reaction from naturalism in a new regional fiction and new historical romances.

D. Regional, historical, and conservatively realistic fiction frequently show some influence of the naturalistic narrative technique and its abandonment of reticence; just as a writer whose philosophy is naturalistic may employ a conservative technique (as did Thomas Hardy).

II. Conservative or "classical" novels, mostly of contemporary life

A. The emphasis is on individual men and women—their struggles, successes, and failures in terms of character and motive—not on man as a physical or a sociological organism. In style there is usually a cultivated, literary manner, not primitivism.

B. ELLEN [Anderson Gholson] GLASGOW (1874-   )

1. Born in Richmond, Virginia, April 22, 1874; privately educated, beginning her "literary work as a rebel against conventions," Miss Glasgow has always endeavored to depict the life of the South truly, realistically, avoiding both "the fabulous Southern hero of the past" and "the fabulous Southern monster of the present." She has classified in three groups what she regards as her most important novels:

2. A survey of the social history of Virginia from 1850 to 1912: In *The Battleground* (1902), *The Deliverance* (1904), *Virginia* (1913), *The Voice of the People* (1900), *The Romance of a Plain Man* (1909), and *Life and Gabriella* (1916), heroes and heroines struggle for business success against social discrimination, or with difficult family conditions. The plots of the earlier novels are sometimes melodramatic, but the characterization is strong. Influence of Dickens and Hardy, especially in the humor.

3. Novels of contemporary urban life: *The Romantic Comedians* (1926), *They Stooped to Folly* (1929), and *The Sheltered Life* (1932) are witty and subtle dramas of personal relationships, with memorable studies of older and younger generations.

4. Novels of contemporary country life: *The Miller of Old Church* (1911), with a complex, Dickens-like plot, dominated by a neurotic woman "invalid"; *Barren Ground* (1925), the moving drama of Dorinda Oakley, who, disappointed in love, fights a winning fight with a "barren" Virginia farm; *Vein of Iron* (1935), powerful

study of three generations of another Scotch-Irish Virginia family, down to post-war days and problems.

5. General estimate

Plots in early novels romantic and "Victorian"; later work also complex and full-bodied, but extremely well-conducted. Excellent characterization throughout, increasing in depth and seriousness; especially good in portraits of elderly men, scheming women, and young women steadfast and heroic. Finely wrought mature style; irony and humor; shrewd judgments of life as it is.

C. WILLA [Sibert] CATHER (1876–   )

1. Born in Winchester, Virginia, December 7, 1876; childhood in Nebraska farm country; graduated, University of Nebraska, 1895. Newspaper work, 1898–1901; travel; associate editor, *McClure's Magazine*, 1906–12.

2. Began literary work with poems, *April Twilights* (1903), and short stories, *The Troll Garden* (1905), mostly on traditional themes. Admiration for Balzac, Longfellow, Henry James, and Sarah Orne Jewett.

3. Her novels of pioneer background—*O Pioneers!* (1913) and *My Antonia* (1918)—are marked by fine understanding of the simple emotions and fundamental conflicts of life, by the powerful figures of her peasant heroines, and by a loose and episodic structure. The same traits appear in *The Song of the Lark* (1915), the struggle toward success as a singer of a small-town girl.

4. Increased power in her later novels, which with change of scene and of protagonist—*The Professor's House* (1925), scene a Middle-Western university; *Death Comes for the Archbishop* (1927), of the pioneer bishop who founded the Catholic diocese of New Mexico in 1848; and *Shadows on the Rock* (1931), laid in seventeenth-century Quebec—still convey a sense of the dignity and significance of life.

5. General estimate

Action in the novels relatively slight and structure often loose; the emphasis is rather upon thoughts and emotions than upon deeds. Special distinction in the creation of characters who are simple but of rich human vitality and wisdom. A style also simple and sincere, often poetical, sometimes commonplace.

D. Satirical realists

1. ZONA GALE [Mrs. William L. Breese] (1874–1938)
   After the romantic and sentimental stories, *Friendship Village* (1908), *Neighborhood Stories* (1914), etc., in *Birth* (1918), *Faint Perfume* (1923), and the famous *Miss Lulu Bett* (1920) she satirizes pettiness and selfishness in family relations.

2. JOHN PHILLIPS MARQUAND (1893–   )
   a) Popular success with magazine stories, and the skilful romances with Eastern background, *Ming Yellow* (1934), *No Hero* (1935), *Thank You, Mr. Moto* (1936), etc.
   b) More serious studies of New England life: class contrasts in *Warning Hill* (1930) and *Haven's End* (1933); reaching distinction in the quietly but profoundly ironic *The Late George Apley* (1937) and *Wickford Point* (1939).

3. LOUIS BROMFIELD (1896–   ) showed gift for satire in *A Good Woman* (1927) and *The Strange Case of Miss Annie Spragg* (1928); but more frequently writes vivid and exciting romances, with excellent characterization and a serious undercurrent, such as *A Modern Hero* (1932) and *The Rains Came* (1937).

E. Sober studies of individual and family problems are found in *The Bent Twig* (1915), *The Brimming Cup* (1921), *The Deepening Stream* (1930), etc., by DOROTHY CANFIELD FISHER [Mrs. John R. Fisher] (1879–   ); in *Years of Grace* (1930), its sequel, *Wisdom's Gate* (1938), and the more powerful *Edna, His Wife* (1935), by MARGARET AYER BARNES [Mrs. Cecil Barnes] (1886–   ); in JOSEPHINE LAWRENCE' tracts on home economics, office work, and parenthood, *If I Have Four Apples* (1935), etc.; and in the Chinese novels by PEARL S. BUCK [Mrs. Richard J. Walsh] (1892–   ), *The Good Earth* (1931), etc.

F. Careful realism in details, sometimes naturalistic in its "primitivism," coupled with real or romantic plots appears in the "new" regional fiction.[1]

1. The East. Maine is the scene in *As the Earth Turns* (1933), etc., by GLADYS HASTY CARROLL (1904–   ) and in *Mary Peters*

[1] See also the regional aspects of the naturalistic and the historical novels below, pp. 94–101.

(1934) and *Silas Crockett* (1935) by MARY ELLEN CHASE (1887–
). Southern New England is the background of WILBUR
DANIEL STEELE'S* *Meat* (1928) and *Sound of Rowlocks* (1938);
and of *The Last Adam* (1933) by JAMES GOULD COZZENS (1903–
).

2. The South has enjoyed a special revival.

    a) JULIA [Mood] PETERKIN [Mrs. William G. Peterkin] (1880–
) has portrayed the negro spirit with convincing realism
in *Black April* (1927), *Scarlet Sister Mary* (1928), and *Bright
Skin* (1932).

    b) ELIZABETH MADOX ROBERTS* (1886–1941) depicted truly yet
poetically the lives and emotions of simple Kentucky folk in
The Time of Man (1926); her plot is melodramatic and ob-
scured by symbolic overtones in *He Sent Forth a Raven* (1935).

    c) MARJORIE KINNAN RAWLINGS (1896–   ) shows sympathy
and understanding in her dramatic stories of the impover-
ished whites of the Florida scrub, *South Moon Under* (1933),
Golden Apples (1935); *The Yearling* (1938) has a simpler plot
and a more moving tenderness.

3. The West and the Southwest

    a) RUTH SUCKOW [Mrs. Ferner Nuhn] (1892–   ) writes of the
ordinary people of Iowa with a quiet understanding like that
of the older chroniclers of New England life in her short
stories, *Country People* (1924), *Iowa Interiors* (1926), etc., and
in her novels, *The Bonney Family* (1928), *The Kramer Girls*
(1930), etc.

    b) Others include PHIL[ip Duffield] STONG (1899–   ) in *State
Fair* (1932), *Career* (1936), etc.; GLENWAY WESCOTT* (1901–
) in *The Apple of the Eye* (1924) and *The Grandmothers*
(1927); and PAUL HORGAN (1903–   ) in his studies of passion and character conflict, *No Quarter Given* (1935), *Main
Line West* (1936), etc.

G. Fantasy—for its own sake or with a "tendency"

1. ROBERT NATHAN (1894–   ), literary heir of F. R. Stockton and
Anatole France, with a gentle intensity and a consciousness of
world-problems besides; writing marked by thoughtfulness, irony,
melancholy, whimsy; style delicate and poetical.

  a) *Road of Ages* (1935), the supposed last journey into exile of
  the Jewish race, a narrative both realistic and symbolic, rises
  above pathos to tragedy.

  b) Lighter and more characteristic are: *The Barley Fields* (col-
  lecting several earlier pieces) (1938), *One More Spring* (1933),
  etc.

2. THORNTON [Niven] WILDER* (1897–   ) has stated modern
   moral problems in terms of past societies, in his exquisitely
   wrought tales, *The Bridge of San Luis Rey* (1927) and *The Woman
   of Andros* (1930); ELINOR WYLIE* [Mrs. William R. Benét]
   (1887–1928), learned, wayward, and exquisite, wrote satirical
   fantasies in a flawless Augustan style somewhat reminiscent of
   Voltaire, Beckford, and Beerbohm—*Jennifer Lorn* (1923), *The
   Venetian Glass Nephew* (1925); *The Orphan Angel* (1926), of Shelley, saved from the sea, making a pilgrimage across America, and
   Mr. Hodge and Mr. Hazard (1928), in ridicule of Victorian stuffi-
   ness; CHRISTOPHER [Darlington] MORLEY* (1890–   ) is play-
   ful or facetious in *When the Blue Begins* (1922), etc.; FREDERICK
   PROKOSCH (1909–   ) shows Occidentals in the East, seeking
   moral escape and meeting their destiny, in his picaresque *The
   Asiatics* (1935) and *The Seven Who Fled* (1937).

III. The Development of Naturalism

A. Data up to the World War: the spread of scientific thought; French
   naturalism—Flaubert, Zola; realism in America—Howells, etc.;
   the "nineties"—Howe, Garland, Crane, etc.; Theodore Dreiser; cf.
   above, pp. 60–62, 66–68, 72.

B. The evolved pattern[1]

  1. Philosophy: (*a*) *scientific determinism*, the force controlling man
     being sociological (heredity and environment), mechanistic (bio-
     chemistry), behaviorist (glands), or fatalistic (blind chance);
     (*b*) *pessimism*, a skeptical view of life as mean or meaningless;
     amorality—where nature has no standards, man has no responsi-
     bility, where life has no meaning, man has no goal but sensation.

  2. Subject-matter: the primitive, the instinctive, the ugly, the mean,

[1] See Parrington, III, 323 ff.; Muller, pp. 159–222.

the vicious; principal characters (*a*) simple, oversimple, non-intellectual or (*b*) sophisticates and neurotics.

3. Technique: (*a*) Impressionism or expressionism; objectivity or autobiography, self-analysis; structural incoherence (form is false to life); slice of life; stream of consciousness. (*b*) Unliterary, unintellectual style, with brutal diction; or subtle, brittle, highly personalized.

4. Naturalism has the merit of breaking with outworn shibboleths and taboos, but the defect of itself presenting a distorted and often unwholesome view of reality.

C. The psychologists

These students of mental states usually combine a philosophic determinism and great frankness of naturalistic detail with a consciously literary form. Their underlying mood is more often romantic than realistic.

1. SHERWOOD ANDERSON* (1876–1941)

a) Influenced by Whitman, Freud, Dreiser; also by GERTRUDE STEIN* (1874–   ), whose expressionistic *Tender Buttons* (1915) roused his enthusiasm; himself influential on younger writers, including Faulkner and Hemingway; all his writing a sort of spiritual autobiography.

b) His constantly repeated theme is the futility of life with the repressions and frustrations which wall it in: through false morality, as in the short stories, in *Many Marriages* (1923) and in *Dark Laughter* (1925); or one's job, as in *Windy McPherson's Son* (1916); or industrialized society plus the hero's maladjusted nature, as in *Marching Men* (1917), *Poor White* (1920), *Beyond Desire* (1932), etc. Escape is sought by flight from society or to sex experience or both; usually in vain.

c) Anderson's strength is his sincere poetic feeling, his sensitive recording of unhappy souls, and an honest simplicity of style. Weaknesses: the psychologically unreal or infantile behavior of his characters; his naïve love of "frankness"; his obsession with a single theme.

2. WILLIAM FAULKNER [Falkner] (1897–   )

a) Born in New Albany, Mississippi; student at University of Mississippi and Oxford University; aviator in World War;

resident of Oxford, Mississippi, the "Jefferson" of the novels; some family history and family portraits also in the novels. Literary influence of Gertrude Stein, James Joyce, Sherwood Anderson.

b) After the typical disillusionment of *Soldiers' Pay* (1926) and the sophisticated *Mosquitoes* (1927), he initiates serious handling of his authentic material in *Sartoris* (1929), the last phase of the Sartoris "cycle."

c) *The Sound and the Fury* (1929), a tale largely "told by an idiot" of the degeneracy of the Compson family through the influence of the post-Civil War environment and the physical taint from a neurotic mother, is in every way typical Faulkner: frustrations, sex complexes, pervasive violence and fear in the theme; stream-of-consciousness technique with kaleidoscopic shifts from one person's consciousness to another's and from one generation in time to another; magnificent style creating moods of horror and pity.

d) *As I Lay Dying* (1930), the journey of a family of poor whites with the mother's dead body, *Sanctuary* (1931), the sensational story of the perverse Temple Drake and the associated group of symbolic grotesques who destroy one another, and *Light in August* (1932), the nightmarish history of a neurotic mulatto, are more clearly told and combine macabre humor with despair.

e) In *Pylon* (1935) and *Absalom! Absalom!* (1936) complex inversion of narrative reappears; the latter novel, however, presents with great power the defeat and destruction of another family group, the Sutphens.

f) Relative clarity and greater normality, with perhaps somewhat diminished force, distinguish *The Unvanquished* (1938), a group of tales which together tell the earlier story of the Sartoris family; and *The Wild Palms* (1939), an experiment in the parallel development of two contrasted themes.

g) At his best Faulkner surpasses all his contemporaries in his depiction of the disintegration of character and the "jungle of the unconscious," with a narrative technique and style perfectly suited to his themes. Too often, however, the author is the victim of his material and his manner.

3. THOMAS [Clayton] WOLFE (1900–1938)
   a) Born at Asheville, North Carolina; A.B., University of North
      Carolina, 1920; A.M., Harvard, 1922; instructor in English,
      New York University, 1924–30. Influenced by Whitman,
      Joyce, Sherwood Anderson; fond of Shakspere and the Bible,
      Burton's *Anatomy*, and Gibbon.
   b) His chief work consists of: four novels, *Look Homeward,
      Angel* (1929), *Of Time and the River* (1935), *The Web and the
      Rock* (1939), and *You Can't Go Home Again* (1940), and a
      volume of sketches and stories, *From Death to Morning* (1935).
      All his fiction is transparently autobiographical.
   c) There is little sign of growth in his work, which, like Ander-
      son's, is marked by a permanent adolescence: the naïveté of
      the cosmic meditations, the introverted, sentimentalized
      heroes, the tremendous violence and verbosity of diction,
      paralysis of selection, amorphousness, and irrelevance. Yet
      he has been described as the greatest novelist of the decade
      because of his Whitman-like sense of America and of hu-
      manity, his ability to reproduce scenes and characters to the
      life, his fecundity, his gusto.
4. Other novelists whose naturalism has a psychological emphasis
   and who often employ the stream-of-consciousness technique:
   FLOYD DELL (1887–   ), whose studies of adolescence in *Moon-
   Calf* (1920), of the adjustment of personalities in marriage in *The
   Briary Bush* (1923), etc., have a romantic coloring; EVELYN SCOTT
   [Mrs. John Metcalfe] (1893–   ), who in *The Narrow House*
   (1921), *Narcissus* (1922), *The Wave* (1929), *Eva Gay* (1933), etc.,
   reveals greater understanding of the new psychology than ability
   to present living characters in an absorbing action and a natural
   style; BEN HECHT (1894–   ), who in *Erik Dorn* (1921) gave an
   excellent study of a morbid literary temperament; F. SCOTT FITZ-
   GERALD* (1896–1940), skilful painter of a neurotic woman in
   Tender Is the Night (1934); CONRAD [Potter] AIKEN* (1889–   ),
   who too scientifically portrays the mind of a philanderer in *Blue
   Voyage* (1927), of a cuckold in *Great Circle* (1933), and a manic
   depressive in *King Coffin* (1935); JULIAN GREEN (1900–   ),
   born and resident in France, disciplined and subtle analyst of in-
   hibited souls in *The Closed Garden* (1927), *The Dark Journey*

(1929), and *The Strange River* (1931); ELIZABETH MADOX ROB-
ERTS,* author of *My Heart and My Flesh* (1927); and KAY BOYLE*
[Mrs. Laurence Vail] (1903–   ), whose mastery of impression-
istic technique and brilliant style do not quite suffice in *Plagued
by the Nightingale* (1931), *Death of a Man* (1936), etc.

5. A more wholesome, even a hopeful, mood dominates some later
studies, such as MILLEN BRAND'S *The Outward Room* (1937),
CLYDE BRION DAVIS'* *The Anointed* (1937), and EDWIN LAN-
HAM'S* *Another Ophelia* (1938).

D. The primitivists, or the "hard-boiled" school

In these authors the harsher, non-intellectual elements of naturalism dominate. Their realism is so extreme (details selected with
such strong bias) as itself to constitute a romanticism.

1. ERNEST HEMINGWAY* (1898–   )

   a) Influenced by the French naturalists and by Dreiser, Sherwood Anderson, Gertrude Stein; also the most conspicuous
   victim of the post-war "psychosis," the disillusionment after
   1919;[1] himself imitated by younger men.

   b) Making his first reputation with short stories, he has written
   two distinguished novels, *A Farewell to Arms* (1929) and *For
   Whom the Bell Tolls* (1940), in which the bareness of the
   naturalistic technique and the underlying skepticism enhance
   the genuinely human tragedy of his principals. In *The Sun
   Also Rises* (1926), post-war France is the setting for Nature's
   grim joke on a nympholept in love with an incapacitated ex-
   soldier; *To Have and Have Not* (1937) is the incoherent epic of
   Harry Morgan, rum-runner and "expensive animal."

   c) General character: simple stories, dramatic and usually in-
   volving violence or despair, about simple-minded people,
   presented with objectivity in a bare, uncolored, unanalytical,
   but highly individual style; characters "sophistically simple,"
   as near as may be to a strictly physiological life. Pessimism less
   pronounced in his latest work.

2. Heirs of the Hemingway manner, with a simplification of the
Hemingway philosophy to mere behaviorism, include: WILLIAM

[1] See below, p. 101.

RILEY BURNETT (1899–   ) in the gangsters of *Little Caesar* (1929), etc.; JAMES MALLAHAN CAIN (1892–   ) in *The Postman Always Rings Twice* (1934) and *Serenade* (1937); JOHN [Henry] O'HARA (1905–   ) in *Appointment in Samarra* (1934), *Butterfield 8* (1935), etc.

3. Strongly influenced by the Hemingway group in choice of subjects and in manner, but with a different outlook:

   a) ERSKINE CALDWELL* (1902–   ) combines harsh naturalism of manner and choice of subnormal characters with an absorption like Faulkner's in the byways of passion and desire. Social pity relieves somewhat the horrible and low in *Tobacco Road* (1932) and *God's Little Acre* (1933).

   b) JAMES THOMAS FARRELL (1904–   ) shows a firm grasp on character, clear moral sense, and indignation at the destructive influences of the slums in the Studs Lonigan trilogy— *Young Lonigan* (1932), *The Young Manhood of Studs Lonigan* (1934), and *Judgment Day* (1935); there is increased humanity but insufficient selection in his O'Neill sequence, *A World I Never Made* (1936) and *No Star Is Lost* (1938).

4. The naturalistic technique has affected other writers whose novels have primarily a social significance, including John Dos Passos, John Steinbeck, John T. McIntyre.[1]

IV. Historical Fiction

A revival in the 1930's, partly for "escape," partly an accompaniment of the "new regionalism" and the stronger national sentiment following the war. It differs from *fin de siècle* historical romance principally in (1) superior documentation, often at the expense of narrative interest, (2) sophistication, which introduces a "debunking" realism of language and behavior.

A. Romances of adventure

   1. KENNETH [Lewis] ROBERTS (1885–   ) wrote with vigor and color of Colonial New England in *Arundel* (1930) and *Rabble in Arms* (1933). In *Northwest Passage* (1937), a story of the expedition against Quebec, he drew a great historical portrait in Colonel Rogers.

[1] See below, pp. 102–4.

2. JAMES BOYD (1888–   ) has ease and sometimes poignancy, with good characterization and sufficient historical background in stories laid in the South from Colonial times to the Civil War—*Drums* (1925), etc.

3. WALTER DUMAX EDMONDS (1903–   ) tells lively, rather loosely unified stories of upstate New York, with good "Dickensish" characters, in *Rome Haul* (1929), etc., but is too documentary and disconnected in *Drums along the Mohawk* (1936); [William] HERVEY ALLEN (1889–   ) with practiced hand combines sex, sentimental philosophy, and a multitude of old situations in *Anthony Adverse* (1933); MARGARET MITCHELL [Mrs. John R. Marsh] in *Gone with the Wind* (1936) has a tale of Southern chivalry in defeat made piquant by a modernistic heroine and a Byronic villain-hero; HAROLD LENOIR DAVIS (1896–   ) has gusto in the picaresque yarn of the Oregon Trail, *Honey in the Horn* (1935).

B. Quieter studies of time and place

1. HERBERT QUICK (1861–1925) wrote of Iowa farmers through a half-century of struggle in *Vandemark's Folly* (1922), *The Hawk-eye* (1923), and *The Invisible Woman* (1924); OLE EDVART RÖLVAAG (1876–   ) with epic scope told of Norwegian pioneers in Dakota in *Giants in the Earth* (1927); EDNA FERBER (1887–   ) shows gift for drama and command of romantic character and background in *Show Boat* (1926), tale of paddle-wheel days on the Mississippi, and *Cimarron* (1929), the theme of which is the opening of Oklahoma; HONORÉ WILLSIE MORROW (1880–1940) is careful and sound in *Benefits Forgot* (1917), *Forever Free* (1927), etc.; RACHEL [Lyman] FIELD [Mrs. Arthur S. Pederson] (1894–   ) has caught the true quality of New England scenes and characters in *Time Out of Mind* (1935) and *All This and Heaven Too* (1938); ESTHER FORBES has shown increasing command of historical narrative in *Miss Marvel* (1935), *Paradise* (1937), etc.

2. Others include: JOHN T. MCINTYRE'S* full-bodied Dickens-like stories of old Philadelphia, *Blowing Weather* (1923), *Shot Towers* (1926), etc.; MARTHA OSTENSO'S *Wild Geese* (1925); ELIZABETH

MADOX ROBERTS'* The Great Meadow (1930), poetic but lacking in events; and FRANCES WINWAR'S dramatic novel of Salem in witchcraft days, Gallows Hill (1937).

V. The Novel of Social Criticism

A. Post-war disillusionment and "debunking"

1. Found early expression in anti-war novels, such as DOS PASSOS'* Three Comrades (1921) and E. E. CUMMINGS'* The Enormous Room (1922). Later examples are THOMAS BOYD'S Through the Wheat (1923), LAURENCE STALLINGS'* Plumes (1924), and FAULKNER'S* Soldiers' Pay.

2. Appeared more comprehensively in such studies of "flaming youth" and "country club society" as the earlier stories and novels of F[rancis] SCOTT [Key] FITZGERALD,* This Side of Paradise (1920), The Beautiful and Damned (1921), Tales of the Jazz Age (1922), and The Great Gatsby (1925); and in Young Man of Manhattan (1930), Don't Ever Leave Me (1935), etc., sophisticated stories of sophisticates by KATHERINE [Ingham] BRUSH [Mrs. Hubert C. Winans].

B. SINCLAIR LEWIS (1885–   )

1. Born in Sauk Center, Minnesota, February 7, 1885; A.B., Yale, 1907; journalist and editor to 1916. Five novels (1914–19) preceded his first popular success with Main Street (1920); awarded Nobel Prize, 1930.

2. In his principal novels various displeasing aspects of American life or character are portrayed with photographic accuracy and satirical pungency: Main Street "debunks" the Middle-Western small town vividly and somewhat tediously. Babbitt (1922) is the satirical epic—unfair but unforgettable—of the "typical" businessman, George F. Babbitt. Arrowsmith (1925), commonly considered his greatest novel, is the story of an idealistic physician-scientist's struggle to be honest and to advance knowledge, when politics and private profit and a rich wife tempt or oppose; idea sustained, but narrative often drags. Dodsworth (1929), built on the conflict between the hero, a retired businessman, and his self-indulgent wife, has less satire and little caricature; it contains his most real and moving characterization.

3. Vigorously written but less successful as art or propaganda are: *Elmer Gantry* (1927), a portrait of an incredibly vicious evangelist; *Ann Vickers* (1933), study of an intelligent woman whose life is a series of unintelligent moral choices; *It Can't Happen Here* (1935), story of when fascism comes to America; etc.

4. General estimate
   a) Work firmly grounded in the life of average Americans; shows ability to reproduce the surfaces of life and speech with extraordinary accuracy; exposes our weaknesses with pungent and sometimes penetrating satire; reflects a fundamentally wholesome liberalism, with hatred of social and political nostrums, isms, and cant.
   b) An admirer of H. G. Wells, he is, like Wells, usually more the journalist than the artist; has no great narrative gift or insight below the surface of character; style commonplace; criticisms not usually constructive.

C. JOHN [Roderigo] DOS PASSOS* (1896–   )
   1. Born in Chicago, January 14, 1896; A.B., Harvard, 1916; war service; travel; newspaper correspondent. Strongly influenced by James Joyce.
   2. Earlier novels depict the aesthete or the man of artistic temper in conflict with a brutal world: the musician in *Three Soldiers* (1921); *Streets of Night* (1923); Jimmy Herf in *Manhattan Transfer* (1925).
   3. His principal novels constitute the most comprehensive depiction in fiction of modern capitalistic society: its confusion, complexity, soullessness; the success of the few men of native power and the barrenness or futility of the lives of ordinary men. Called "mass novels" because individuals are incidental to the "social" theme, they develop a special "flicker" technique (snapshots here and there—discontinuous narrative), which is effective and has been widely imitated. These novels include:
      a) *Manhattan Transfer*, picture of the economic wastage and spiritual chaos of metropolitan New York.
      b) *The 42d Parallel* (1930), *Nineteen Nineteen* (1931), and *The Big Money* (1936)—an American trilogy reissued as *U.S.A.*

(1938)—state the dilemma of the common man in terms nearly acceptable to the "literary Left" (proletarians).

4. *Adventures of a Young Man* (1939), story of a young liberal who works with union organizers in the mining regions and loses his life through Loyalist Party factionalism in Spain, constitutes a severe criticism of Communist Party methods; in technique a return to the unity of a single protagonist.

5. General estimate: Distinguished for seriousness of theme, comprehensive grasp and forceful analysis of modern society, a rapid, plain, "realistic" style; vague in conclusions and weak in the central function of the novelist, character portrayal.

D. JOHN STEINBECK* (1902–   )

1. First success with *Tortilla Flat* (1935), the comic exploits of a group of irresponsible Southern California *paisanos;* fame extended by his prize-winning long short story, *Of Mice and Men* (1937).

2. Two important novels of social significance: *In Dubious Battle* (1936), of the bloody struggle between Communist-organized apple-pickers and the growers' association; and *Grapes of Wrath* (1939), which follows the fortunes of the Joad family, Oklahoma share croppers forced off their land, journeying to California and suffering from low wages, violence, and intimidation.

3. Work marked by naturalism in narrative details and in style, admirable economy and dramatic force, sharp characterization, indignation and human sympathy without a dogmatic proletarianism.

E. Proletarian novelists

1. Among those apparently fully accepted as fictional spokesmen for the party are: ROBERT EMMETT CANTWELL (1908–   ), author of *Land of Plenty* (1934), on a strike in a veneer factory; ALBERT HALPER (1904–   ), who, after the vivid, unpartisan, and rather confused picture of the troubled lives of the inhabitants of a city block in *Union Square* (1933), described industrial stresses with intimate understanding and human feeling in *The Foundry* (1934) and repeated himself, with change of scene, in *The Chute* (1937); JOSEPHINE HERBST [Mrs. John Herrmann] (1897–   ), influ-

enced by Dos Passos, who portrays with power and passionate conviction the supposed collapse of capitalism in her trilogy *Pity Is Not Enough* (1933), *The Executioner Waits* (1934), and *Rope of Gold* (1939).

2. Authors sometimes approved, sometimes criticized for imperfect understanding of or incomplete commitment to the radical philosophy, include: ERSKINE CALDWELL*; JAMES T. FARRELL*; WALDO FRANK (1889–   ), author of *City Block* (1922), and of *The Death and Birth of David Markand* (1934), the hero of which, escaping from his servitude to wealth, finds a rebirth in Communism.

F   Other writers who are concerned with the problems of contemporary society include: THOMAS SIGISMUND STRIBLING (1881–   ), who shows skill in story-telling and characterization and sympathy with the underdog in his earlier stories of racial and economic problems of the South, such as *Birthright* (1921), *Teeftallow* (1926), and *The Store* (1932); CHARLES GILMAN NORRIS (1881–   ), who systematically but not subtly deals with divorce in *Brass* (1921), feminism in *Bread* (1923), birth control in *Seed* (1930), etc.; PAUL [Eliot] GREEN* (1894–   ), who in *This Body the Earth* (1935) exhibits the plight of the Southern share croppers, as does EDWIN LANHAM* (1904–   ) in the less doctrinaire and more moving *The Stricklands* (1939); JOHN T. McINTYRE,* who reveals the humanity of characters close to the underworld in *Steps Going Down* (1936); TESS SLESINGER [Mrs. Frank Davis] (1905–   ), who in *The Unpossessed* (1934), with Joycean technique, portrays a "depression" society, decadent, fearful of collapse, and afraid of life; and THOMAS BELL (1910–   ), whose hero and heroine in *All Brides Are Beautiful* (1936) wring from this same economic stress a difficult happiness.

VI. The Short Story

A. Tendencies: to break down the strict rules of form and structure in the interest of a greater truth to life; less emphasis on "local color" regionalism and increased social significance; in general, close parallelism between novel and short story in subjects, structure, and style.

B. Romantic background with realism of detail appears in: WILBUR
DANIEL STEELE* (1886–   ), author of *Land's End* (1918), *The
Shame Dance* (1923), *The Man Who Saw through Heaven* (1927),
etc.; EDNA FERBER,* author of *Roast Beef Medium* (1913), *Cheerful,
by Request* (1918), etc.; STEPHEN VINCENT BENÉT* (1898–   ),
author of *Thirteen O'Clock* (1937), etc.

C. Literary finish and sophistication are conspicuous in: KATHERINE
FULLERTON GEROULD *(1879–   ), author of *Vain Oblations* (1914),
Valiant Dust (1922); KAY BOYLE,* author of *Wedding Day* (1931),
The First Lover (1933), *The White Horses of Vienna* (1936); DOROTHY
[Rothschild] PARKER [Mrs. Alan Campbell] (1893–   ), author of
Laments for the Living (1930) and *After Such Pleasures* (1933);
KATHERINE ANNE PORTER (1894–   ), author of *Flowering Judas*
(1935); and TESS SLESINGER,* author of *Time: The Present* (1936).

D. Naturalistic technicians

   1. ERNEST HEMINGWAY* has found in the short story his most
   congenial literary form and in it has been most influential. Con-
   spicuously successful are "My Old Man" in *In Our Time* (1924),
   "The Killers" in *Men without Women* (1927), "The Snows of
   Kilimanjaro" in *Green Hills of Africa* (1935).

   2. JOHN T. FARRELL* in *Calico Shoes* (1934) and *Guillotine Party*
   (1935) and JOHN STEINBECK* in *The Long Valley* (1938) show
   the same tendency toward social criticism as in their novels;
   WILLIAM SAROYAN (1908–   ) in *The Daring Young Man on the
   Flying Trapeze* (1934), etc., artfully professing no art at all, is
   occasionally poignant in depiction of the immigrant consciousness.

   3. More violent social criticism is expressed in ERSKINE CALD-
   WELL'S* *Kneel to the Rising Sun* (1935), ALBERT MALTZ' *The Way
   Things Are* (1938), and the stories by two negro writers, *The Way
   of White Folks* (1934) by LANGSTON HUGHES (1902–   ) and
   Uncle Tom's Children (1938) by RICHARD WRIGHT.

E. The long short story (improperly, "novella") shows increased popularity. It has been used with distinction by many writers, including [Brian Oswald] DONN BYRNE* (1889–1928) in his poetic Irish
story-teller's version of an old adventure, *Messer Marco Polo* (1921);

GLENWAY WESCOTT* in the Jamesian *The Pilgrim Hawk* (1941);
MACKINLAY KANTOR (1904–   ), author of the graceful and moving *Long Remember* (1934), *The Voice of Bugle Ann* (1935), etc.;
LOUIS BROMFIELD* in *Here Today* (1934); EDNA FERBER* in *No-
body's in Town* (1937); JOHN STEINBECK* in *Of Mice and Men*
(1937); KATHERINE ANNE PORTER* in *Pale Horse, Pale Rider* (1939).

F. Short stories linked by one or more common characters so that a
loosely organized novel sometimes results are found in EDNA FERB-
ER'S* *Emma McChesney & Co.* (1915); in DONN BYRNE'S* *The Wind
Bloweth* (1922) and *Destiny Bay* (1928); in *Polished Ebony* (1919),
etc., by OCTAVUS ROY COHEN (1891–   ); in *Guys and Dolls* (1932),
etc., glimpses of a stylized underworld by [Alfred] DAMON RUNYON
(1884–   ); in JOHN STEINBECK'S* *Tortilla Flat* and WILLIAM
FAULKNER'S* *The Unvanquished*.

THE DRAMA SINCE THE WAR

I. General Tendencies

A. Tendencies of the first decade of the century (cf. p. 83, IV) continued. Decline of the commercial theater and breakup of the great
producing systems, because of increased cost of touring and compe-
tition of the movies. Continued growth of amateur and semi-professional groups throughout the country, some attaining distinction and influence, such as the Provincetown Players, the Washington Square Players, and the [North] Carolina Playmakers; professional organizations with special programs, like the Theatre Guild
and the Group Theatre of New York, and Gilmour Brown's Pasa-
dena Community Playhouse. The Federal Theatre Project (1936–
39), primarily a "relief" measure for out-of-work dramatists, actors,
and technicians, provided in many communities opportunity for
valuable experimentation with classical and modern plays, and by
its low admission charges restored the theater to the general public.
Latterly, a few leading actors have resumed country-wide tours with
some success.

B. In staging, the reaction against a literal realism led to the modern
"expressionist" or "symbolic" settings and a selective or suggestive

realism; influence of the "camera eye" of the movies. Important scenic artists include Robert Edmond Jones, Norman Bel Geddes, Lee Simonson, and Jo Mielziner.

C. In all the better plays of the contemporary theater drama and literature again draw together; influence of Professor G. P. Baker, whose "47 Workshop" was the first significant contribution of the colleges to the art of the theater; revival of poetic drama. In themes, mood, and language plays parallel the traits of fiction: the new psychology; naturalistic language, especially in plays of social revolt; release from old taboos in subject matter. A seriousness, intelligence, and vitality not equaled in the previous history of the American drama.

II. Eugene Gladstone O'Neill* (1888–   )

A. Born, New York City, October 16, 1888, son of James O'Neill, the distinguished actor; studied at Princeton and under Baker at Harvard; varied experiences as seaman, in jobs in South America, as newspaper reporter and resident of Greenwich Village; joined Provincetown Players in 1916. Among those who have exerted an influence on his thought or his dramatic technique are: Aeschylus, Nietzsche, Ibsen, Strindberg, Freud, James Joyce. Awarded Nobel Prize for literature in 1936.

B. Plays mainly realistic in mood and technique, with some naturalism in detail.
   1. *Beyond the Horizon* (1920)[1] infuses with poetic feeling the realistic tragedy of two brothers in love with the same woman.
   2. *Anna Christie* (1921) is a violent yet tender tale of regeneration through love; scenes and characters from the water front. Compare for materials the early one-act plays; see above, p. 84.
   3. *Ah, Wilderness!* (1933) represents a return to traditional forms and the mood of comedy.

C. Plays increasingly experimental or expressionist in technique; themes of inner conflict, neuroses, and maladjustments.
   1. *The Emperor Jones* (1920) is the finely imaginative tragedy of the Pullman-car porter made "Emperor" who is destroyed by fear.

[1] Unless otherwise noted, in the drama section the dates of first production are given.

2. *All God's Chillun Got Wings* (1924), superficially a tragedy of mis-
cegenation, is essentially the sympathetic story of a young negro's
defeat in a land of strong racial feeling, as he struggles to become
a lawyer.

3. *Desire under the Elms* (1924), powerful, grimly realistic, technically clever melodrama of a decadent New England family group.

4. *Strange Interlude* (1928) is a Freudian drama of the "unconscious," in two Parts and nine Acts, in which the actual dialogue
is continuously interspersed with "asides" revealing the thoughts
and unconscious reactions of the characters. (Compare with the
two or more simultaneous planes of narrative in Faulkner's
novels.)

5. *Mourning Becomes Electra* (1931) presents in the Mannon family
a modern counterpart to the *Oresteia*, the fatal action interpreted
in terms of mother and father "fixations." The long and compli-
cated action of the "trilogy" is conducted with superb sense of
theater and emotional sincerity. By many thought O'Neill's
greatest play.

D. Symbolism dominates *The Hairy Ape* (1922), a tragedy of man not
yet successful in "working out the beast"; *Marco Millions* (written
1925; prod. 1928), a satire in which Marco Polo stands for the modern businessman; *The Great God Brown* (1926), in which with somewhat debatable success all the characters are made to appear in two
guises, with and without masks, to symbolize the contrast between
the real natures of men and the role they play to the world; and the
three plays which move from the scientific modern view of life's
triumph over death to a mystical Catholicism, *Lazarus Laughed*
(1928), *Dynamo* (1929), and *Days without End* (1934).

E. General estimate
  1. The leading playwright of our time: sure sense of theater, in-
  ventiveness in matters of technique, freedom from bondage to
  tradition.
  2. His place in dramatic literature still to be defined.
    a) It is objected that his plays show triteness, shallowness, and
    confusion of thought. This is partly because he has been feel-
    ing his way toward a philosophy; partly because his style is

less sure on the level of "poetic" emotion than in realistic and vernacular dialogue.

b) His mysticism, which leads inevitably to a sincere not meretricious symbolism, annoys the confirmed rationalist.

c) His work is distinguished by seriousness, dignity, and great emotional and imaginative force. Attempting to recapture the mood of Greek tragedy for a modern theater—stating the dilemma of man and his fate in terms of psychological compulsions and frustrations—he sometimes attains a classical austerity of horror and terror; sometimes the effect fails to rise above the grotesque or pathological.

III. Maxwell Anderson (1888–   )

A. Born, Atlantic, Pennsylvania, December 15, 1888; degrees from University of North Dakota and Stanford University; teacher; newspaper reporter and editorial writer, San Francisco and New York, until 1924.

B. Collaborated plays

1. With LAURENCE STALLINGS* (1894–   ) he wrote the "debunking" realistic war play, *What Price Glory* (1924), a romantic historical play about Andrew Jackson, *First Flight* (1925), and a pirate melodrama, *The Buccaneer* (1925).

2. With HAROLD HICKERSON he wrote *Gods of the Lightning* (1928), indignantly dramatizing the Sacco-Vanzetti case.

C. Success came with two plays of contemporary life, *Saturday's Children* (1927), a sympathetic study of young married people, and *Both Your Houses* (1933), a boisterous, disillusioned caricature of congressional venality.

D. Poetic dramas[1]

1. In *Elizabeth the Queen* (1930) and *Mary of Scotland* (1933) historical truth is strained, but the story is handled with romantic warmth and the contrasting characters are well drawn. Technique rather too Elizabethan.

2. *Valley Forge* (1934) endeavors with imperfect success to assimilate

[1] For Mr. Anderson's credo see his Preface to *Winterset*.

a rather rowdy realism to poetic drama by use of a roughened and irregular versification.

3. In *Winterset* (1935) the Sacco-Vanzetti theme provides the background for the tragedy of a son seeking to clear his father's name; in it love and sacrifice are the solvents of hatred and fear. With much of the melodramatic and coincidental, the play is lifted into romantic tragedy by the poetry and the mood; successful verse tragedy on a modern theme.

4. In 1936–37 three plays wholly or mainly in verse were produced, *High Tor* (1937), an effective, skeptical fantasy of the Adirondacks, and two rather verbose and rhetorical tragedies, *Wingless Victory* (1936) and *The Masque of Kings* (1937).

E. Later works are *The Star Wagon* (1938), a fantasy, the clever musical comedy, *Knickerbocker Holiday* (1938), which like *Both Your Houses* and *The Masque of Kings* mocks idealism and the possibility of social or political reform, and *Key Largo* (1939).

F. General estimate

Great technical skill, serious artistry; important work in the poetic drama. In tolerance and comprehensiveness of view still short of the finest art.

IV. Other Writers of Verse Dramas

A. EDNA ST. VINCENT MILLAY* (1892–   ) followed a group of early plays—most important the one-act satire on war, *Aria da Capo* (1919), and a drama of the Middle Ages, *The Lamp and the Bell* (1921)—with *The King's Henchman* (1927), a lyrical tragedy based on a tenth-century theme, composed as the libretto of an opera, but drama in its own right.

B. ARCHIBALD MACLEISH* (1892–   ) in *Panic* (1935) uses the banking crisis of 1933 as the basis for a symbolic and rhapsodic lyrical drama on the impending collapse of our economic and social order; other current themes are similarly treated in his short plays for the radio, *The Fall of the City* (1937) and *Air Raid* (1938).

C. THOMAS STEARNS ELIOT* (1888–   ) commemorates the death of Thomas à Becket in *Murder in the Cathedral* (1935) and attempts an Aeschylean tragedy in modern dress in *The Family Reunion*

(1939). In both, there is slightness of action, weak characterization, and failure to bridge the gap between poetry and life—largely compensated by the qualities which give distinction to his poetry.

V. The Drama of Character Conflicts, Mainly from Contemporary Life

A. SUSAN GLASPELL* [Mrs. Norman H. Matson] (1882–   ) studies woman's influence on the lives of others in *Bernice* (1919), *The Verge* (1921), and the Pulitzer Prize play *Alison's House* (1930), a delicate and sensitive work which drew some suggestions from the life of Emily Dickinson.

B. SAMUEL NATHANIEL BEHRMAN (1893–   ), a brilliant writer of comedy of manners, at its best fittingly called "high comedy"; more inventive, versatile, and witty than Barry and Howard, equal to Sherwood in literary tact and sense of character and with as clear an awareness of the forces of change threatening the society he depicts with unflinching yet sympathetic irony.

   1. After several moderate successes, including *Brief Moment* (1932), he attained general recognition with *Biography* (1932), clever story of the "liberated" and humorous artist-heroine who makes emotional havoc in the lives of men.

   2. *Rain from Heaven* (1934), under cover of the swift and adroit drawing-room comedy—centering in another witty and wise heroine, Lady Lael Wyngate—satirizes the fear, intolerance, and greed which encourage a betrayal of democracy. His most important play.

   3. In *End of Summer* (1936) and *Wine of Choice* (1938) the detail is equally skilful but the total effect less significant.

C. ROBERT EMMET SHERWOOD (1896–   ), with a distinguished literary gift, lively humorous perceptions, and increasing control of situations of comedy and melodrama and sincerity of characterization, employs romantic materials for the conveying of an essentially serious liberal criticism of our world.[1]

   1. *The Road to Rome* (1927) interprets the turning-point of Hannibal's career as the replacing of materialistic by human values, in a clever, modernistic, superficially naughty play of strong action and sharp, broad characterization.

[1] See his prefaces to *The Road to Pome* and *Reunion in Vienna*.

2. *Reunion in Vienna* (1932) turns a satiric eye upon post-war central Europe and the new psychology; *The Petrified Forest* (1934) with consummate skill employs gangster melodrama at a desert gas station for the satirical portrayal of characters "petrified," out of touch with reality; *Idiot's Delight* (1935) with a similar irony combines comedy of character and the grim outburst of the "next" World War.

3. In *Abe Lincoln in Illinois* (1938), surpassing his previous successes, he returns to historical drama with a clearly underscored liberal message for today. The episodic structure is unified by the masterly portrait of Lincoln, whose inner struggles provide the necessary dramatic conflict.

D. PHILIP BARRY (1896–   ) has written many comedies with great technical skill in control of situation, bright and often moving dialogue, and basic seriousness. Limitations: a sameness in the types of characters and conflicts (young people in love or married, disturbed by the issue created by one's art, an infidelity or the suspicion of it, love of money, incompatability, etc.); also sometimes confusion in the working-out of the problem, which may be stated logically and solved emotionally. His best plays include: *Holiday* (1928), a long one-act symbolic play *Hotel Universe* (1930), *The Animal Kingdom* (1932), and *Here Come the Clowns* (1938). Among others are *You and I* (1923), *In a Garden* (1925), *Paris Bound* (1927), *Tomorrow and Tomorrow* (1931).

E. SIDNEY [Coe] HOWARD* (1891–1939)

1. The early verse tragedy, *Swords* (1921), was followed by romantic dramas, *Bewitched* (1924) (in collaboration with EDWARD SHELDON*), and the Pulitzer Prize play, *They Knew What They Wanted* (1924), the Tristram theme transferred to the vineyards of California.

2. Realistic and convincing characteristizations are found in the loosely organized tragedy, *Lucky Sam McCarver* (1925) and in *Ned McCobb's Daughter* (1926); there is excellent theater with uneven characterization in the popular study of a possessive mother, *The Silver Cord* (1926); scientific research triumphs over yellow fever in *Yellowjack* (1928).

F. Others who have won distinction in one or more plays
  1. GEORGE S. KAUFMAN (1889–   ) has demonstrated his clever-
     ness and versatility in a long series of collaborated comedies
     including *Dulcy* (1921), *To the Ladies* (1922), *Merton of the Movies*
     (1922), and *Beggar on Horseback* (1924) with MARC CONNELLY*;
     Minick (1924), *The Royal Family* (1927), *Dinner at Eight* (1932),
     and *Stage Door* (1936) with EDNA FERBER*; *Once in a Lifetime*
     (1930) and *You Can't Take It with You* (1936) with MOSS HART.
  2. MARC [Marcus Cook] CONNELLY (1890–   ), besides his col-
     laboration with Kaufman, wrote the Pulitzer Prize play which
     portrays with imaginative sympathy though a little sophistically
     the negro's anthropomorphic heaven, *The Green Pastures* (1930).
  3. GEORGE KELLY (1887–   ), beginning with one-act plays like
     Finders-Keepers (pub. 1925), reproduces with uncanny accuracy
     human failings and foibles in *The Show-Off* (1924), *Craig's Wife*
     (1925), *Daisy Mayme* (1926), *Philip Goes Forth* (1931), etc.
  4. LILLIAN HELLMAN (1905–   ) shows technical skill, command of
     character, range of mood, and moral indignation in *The Children's
     Hour* (1934) and *The Little Foxes* (1938).
  5. THORNTON WILDER'S* *Our Town* (1937) is a successful attempt
     to suggest the general in the particular, the lot of mankind in
     moments of the life of Grover's Corners; effect of generalization
     helped by discarding scenery.

VI. Plays of Social Criticism and Propaganda
  A. The development of a "social theater"
    1. Promoted by general turn to realism and by the experimentalism
       of the "new" theater; since the war a large proportion of the plays
       containing social criticism have been written by members of a
       doctrinaire group with a radical social philosophy.
    2. In the contemporary theater plays of social criticism are often
       experimental in technique; the one-act play survives principally
       as a vehicle for theses.

  B. The moderates
    1. ELMER L. RICE (1892–   ). *The Adding Machine* (1923) em-
       ploys expressionist symbolism, with suggestions from Freud and
       Joyce, in the exposure of man's degeneracy in a machine civiliza-

tion; less mannered and more humanly affecting is the realistic slice of life in the "near-slums" of New York, *Street Scene* (1929), winner of the Pulitzer Prize. More violent are the undiscriminating general attacks on capitalism in *We, the People* (1933), and on Hitlerism in *Judgment Day* (1934).

2. PAUL [Eliot] GREEN* (1894–   )

   a) Early one-act plays in which the comedy and tragedy of negro life are set forth with power and sympathy: *White Dresses* (1920; published with other short plays as *Lonesome Road*, 1926). *In Abraham's Bosom* (1926), expanded from two short plays, is on the tragic struggle of a mulatto to rise and to serve his people.

   b) The poor whites of the Carolinas are the theme of such short plays as *The Last of the Louries* (1920), of an outlaw gang; *Fixin's* (1924), of tenant farmers; and *Hymn to the Rising Sun* (1935), bitterly realistic indictment of the treatment of convict gangs.

   c) *The House of Connelly* (1931) is an admirable study of a decaying "aristocratic" family on an old plantation to which new life comes by a marriage into the "poor white" class. His gift for reproducing poetically the rhythms of speech is conspicuous here.

3. SIDNEY KINGSLEY (1907–   ) in *Dead End* (1935) is grimly realistic; his Pulitzer Prize play, *Men in White* (1933), is a well-written melodrama of hospital life.

C. The radicals

1. CLIFFORD ODETS (1906–   ) attained distinction with his violent and overdrawn but powerful and sincere short plays, *Waiting for Lefty* (1935), on a taxicab strike, and the anti-fascist *Till the Day I Die* (1935). In his first full-length play, *Awake and Sing* (1935), he showed the impact of present conditions on the three generations of a New York Jewish family. *Golden Boy* (1937), tragedy of a young man who sacrifices a musical career and becomes a pugilist to win money and fame, shows Odets' mastery of dialogue but is not logically worked out; like *Rocket to the Moon* (1938) it is relatively trivial in theme.

2. Others: JOHN HOWARD LAWSON (1895–   ), author of *Processional* (1925); ALBERT MALTZ*, author of *Peace on Earth* (1933); IRWIN SHAW, author of the one-act *Bury the Dead* (1936) and the much finer full-length play *The Gentle People* (1939).

POETRY

I. General Tendencies

Previous movements continue: opposition of old and new techniques, of pessimism and optimism, of objective and psychological realities. The 1920's predominantly radical and pessimistic; the 1930's increasingly conservative and hopeful.

II. Traditional Lyric and Narrative Poets

A. ROBERT [Lee] FROST (1875–   ), our principal living poet, in short lyrics and longer narrative poems of the New England countryside presents the "mingled web" of life with simplicity, humorous realism, and wisdom. Principal volumes: *North of Boston* (1914), *Mountain Interval* (1916), *New Hampshire* (1923), *West-running Brook* (1928), *A Further Range* (1936).

B. EDNA ST. VINCENT MILLAY* [Mrs. Eugen Jan Boissevain] (1892–   ) gives to personal emotion intense but not flawless lyrical expression in *Renascence* (1917), *The Harp-Weaver* (1923), *Fatal Interview* (sonnets) (1931), etc.; more range, more thought, less passion are in MARK VAN DOREN'S (1894–   ) *Spring Thunder* (1924), *A Winter Diary* (1935), etc.; an elfin intellectuality and brilliance of form in ELINOR WYLIE'S* *Black Armour* (1923), *Trivial Breath* (1928), and *Angels and Earthly Creatures* (1929); power but uncertain taste in *Sunrise Trumpets* (1924), etc., of JOSEPH AUSLANDER (1897–   ); simple feeling in *Man with a Bull-Tongue Plow* (1934), by JESSE STUART (1907–   ); a tortured intelligence in *Two Lives* (1925) of WILLIAM ELLERY LEONARD (1876–   ).

C. Narrative gifts mark *John Brown's Body* (1928) and *Ballads and Poems* (1931) of STEPHEN VINCENT BENÉT (1898–   ); and *Each to the Other* (1939) of CHRISTOPHER LA FARGE (1897–   ).

III. The Modernists

A. [John] ROBINSON JEFFERS (1887–   )

   1. Influenced by English Romanticists; by Rossetti, Swinburne; by Eugene O'Neill; by Freud; also probably by Greek drama and decadent French Naturalists. Themes involve constant physical and spiritual violences—rape, incest, bestiality, murder, suicide—the symbols of a vague nihilistic criticism of human society.

   2. In spite of melodrama and morbid repetitiousness such poems as "The Tower beyond Tragedy" (1925), *Roan Stallion* (1925), *The Women at Point Sur* (1927) and *Give Your Heart to the Hawks* (1933) are redeemed by narrative stride and frequent brilliancy of imagery.

B. Experimental lyricists

   1. E[dward] E[stlin] CUMMINGS (1894–   ) shows genuine lyrical power and fundamental sincerity in his best pieces, though postwar pessimism, eroticism, and dadaist fancies in diction and typography are too conspicuous; see *XLI Poems* (1925), *Is 5* (1926), etc., or *Collected Poems* (1938).

   2. Others include: WALLACE STEVENS (1879–   ), author of *Harmonium* (1923), *The Man with the Blue Guitar* (1937), etc.; OGDEN NASH (1902–   ), masterly ironist in *Hard Lines* (1931), etc.; as well as Crane, Gregory, MacLeish, and Williams.

C. The metaphysicals

   1. Here the influence of French Symbolists, of the Imagists, and of early metaphysical poets like John Donne, along with the postwar neurosis, unite in promoting a poetry of intellectual subtleties, erudite allusions, purely personal imagery (hence, "private meanings"), and skeptic irony.

   2. T. S. ELIOT* (cf. above, p. 80), passing from Imagist to Metaphysical with *The Waste Land*, continues with skepticism changing to faith between "The Hollow Men" (1925) and *Ash-Wednesday* (1930).

   3. Most successful today are: JOHN CROWE RANSOME (1888–   ), witty and sustained stylist, in *Chills and Fever* (1924), *Two Gentlemen in Bonds* (1926), etc.; WILLIAM CARLOS WILLIAMS (1883–   ), the neo-Imagist, in *Kora in Hell* (1920), *Spring and*

Ale (1923), *Collected Poems* (1938); and the intense, lyric mysticism of LÉONIE ADAMS [Mrs. William Troy] (1899–   ), in *High Falcon* (1929), etc.

4. Others include: [Harold] HART CRANE (1899–1932), author of the obscurely symbolic *The Bridge* (1929); ALLEN [John Orley] TATE (1899–   ), too purely "metaphysical" in *Mr. Pope and Other Poems* (1928), etc.; DONALD [Grady] DAVIDSON (1893–   ), author of *The Tall Men* (1927), etc.

IV. The Social-minded

A. ARCHIBALD MACLEISH* (1892–   )
   1. Earlier poems romantic and touched with post-war nostalgia, as in *Streets in the Moon* (1926) and *The Hamlet of A. MacLeish* (1928). Gift of melodious verse and sharply personal imagery.
   2. From *New Found Land* [i.e., America] (1930), through the Mexican epic, *Conquistador* (1932), *Public Speech* (1936), and the verse plays, he expresses with growing clearness the faith of liberal democratic society.

B. Positions further "left" are taken by HORACE [Victor] GREGORY (1898–   ) in *Chelsea Rooming House* (1930), *No Retreat* (1933), and the more hopeful *Chorus for Survival* (1935); KENNETH FEARING (1902–   ) in *Angel Arms* (1929), *Dead Reckoning* (1938), etc.; MURIEL RUKEYSER (1913–   ), in *Theory of Flight* (1935) and *U.S. 1* (1938).

ESSAYS AND MISCELLANEOUS PROSE

I. General Tendencies

Pronounced improvement in the literary form of even ephemeral writing; waning popularity of the light essay; attack on the purely aesthetic approach to criticism.

II. Literary Personal Essays

Mainly survivors from an older generation, this group includes CHARLES HALL GRANDGENT (1862–1939), author of the genial and learned *Getting a Laugh* (1924), *Prunes and Prism* (1928), *The New World*

(1929), etc.; GEORGE SANTAYANA (1863–   ), master of subtle perceptions in *Little Essays* (1920), *Soliloquies in England* (1922), *Obiter Scripta* (1936), etc.; LOGAN PEARSALL SMITH* (1865–   ), author of *Trivia* (1902), *More Trivia* (1921), *On Reading Shakespeare* (1933), *Reperusals and Recollections* (1937), etc.; KATHERINE FULLERTON GEROULD,* pungent critic of mankind in *Modes and Morals* (1919) and *Ringside Seats* (1937); CHRISTOPHER MORLEY,* author of *Shandygaff* (1918), *The Powder of Sympathy* (1923), *Internal Revenue* (1933), etc.

III. Autobiographical Works

The many writers whose personal records cast valuable light not only on themselves but on their times include: IDA MINERVA TARBELL (1857–   ) in *All in the Day's Work* (1939); BLISS PERRY* in *And Gladly Teach* (1935); EDITH WHARTON* in *A Backward Glance* (1934); LOGAN PEARSALL SMITH* in *Unforgotten Years* (1939); [Joseph] LINCOLN STEFFENS (1866–1936) in *Autobiography* (3 vols., 1931); GERTRUDE STEIN* (1874–   ) in *Autobiography of Alice B. Toklas* (1933) and *Everybody's Autobiography* (1937); CLARENCE [Shepard] DAY (1874–1935) in *Life with Father* (1935) and *Life with Mother* (1937); SHERWOOD ANDERSON* in *A Story-Teller's Story* (1924); HENRY SEIDEL CANBY* (1878–   ) in *The Age of Confidence* (1934) and *Alma Mater* (1936); MARY HEATON VORSE in *A Footnote to Folly* (1935); MABEL [Ganson] DODGE LUHAN (1879–   ) in *Intimate Memories* (4 vols., 1933–37); LUDWIG LEWISOHN (1883–   ) in *Upstream* (1923); CARL VAN DOREN* (1885–   ) in *Three Worlds* (1936); ANNE MORROW LINDBERGH (1906–   ) in *North to the Orient* (1935) and *Listen! the Wind* (1938).

IV. Literary and Social Criticism

All are aware of the changing spiritual climate of the world in the present century. Shifts in the position of individual critics make the grouping sometimes tentative.

A. The conservative position is represented by NORMAN FOERSTER (1887–   ), defender, after More and Babbitt, of the "new humanism," in *American Criticism* (1928) and *Toward Standards* (1931); and by THOMAS STEARNS ELIOT* in *The Sacred Wood* (1920), *For Lancelot Andrewes* (1928), and *Essays Ancient and Modern* (1936).

B. Prophets of change were: RANDOLPH BOURNE (1886–1918), in *The History of a Literary Radical* (1920), and especially VERNON LOUIS PARRINGTON (1871–1929) in *Main Currents in American Thought* (3 vols., 1927–30).

C. A moderate position is maintained by: PERCY HOLMES BOYNTON (1875–   ) in *Some Contemporary Americans* (1924), *The Challenge of Modern Criticism* (1931), etc.; HENRY SEIDEL CANBY* in *Definitions* (2 series, 1922, 1924), etc.; MAX EASTMAN (1883– .) in *The Literary Mind* (1931) and *The Enjoyment of Laughter* (1936); CARL VAN DOREN* in *Many Minds* (1924), etc.; VAN WYCK BROOKS (1886–   ) in *America's Coming of Age* (1918), *Emerson and Others* (1927), *The Flowering of New England* (1936), and *New England: Indian Summer* (1940); LEWIS MUMFORD (1895–   ) in *The Golden Day* (1926), *The Culture of Cities* (1938), and *Faith for Living* (1940); EDMUND WILSON (1895–   ) in *Axel's Castle* (1931) and *The Triple Thinkers* (1938); and MALCOLM COWLEY (1898–   ) in *Exile's Return* (1934) and *After the Genteel Tradition* (1937).

D. The radical position is occupied by a diminishing group, among whom are, or have been, GRANVILLE HICKS (1901–   ), author of *The Great Tradition* (1933); BERNARD SMITH (1906–   ), author of the penetrating *Forces in American Criticism* (1939); KENNETH BURKE (1897–   ), author of *Counterstatement* (1931) and *Permanence and Change* (1935).

V. General Commentators

In an area where the bounds of "literature" are vague, there may be mentioned, aside from works of formal history, JAMES TRUSLOW ADAMS (1878–   ) in *The Tempo of Modern Life* (1931); WALTER LIPPMANN (1889–   ), author of *A Preface to Morals* (1929), *The Method of Freedom* (1934), *The Good Society* (1937), etc.; DOROTHY THOMPSON [Mrs. Sinclair Lewis] (1894–   ), author of *Dorothy Thompson's Political Guide* (1938) and *Let the Record Speak* (1939).

APPENDIX CHRONOLOGICAL TABLES

I. AMERICAN HISTORY

THE COLONIAL PERIOD

1607 Jamestown founded
1620 Plymouth Colony founded
1621 New York settled by the Dutch
1630 Massachussets Bay Colony founded
1636 Harvard College founded
     Providence founded
1637 Pequot War
     Anne Hutchinson banished

1639 Printing Press established in Cambridge
1656–61 Persecution of the Quakers
1675–78 King Philip's War
1689–97 King William's War
1692 Salem witchcraft trials
1702–13 Queen Anne's War
1744–48 King George's War
1754–63 French and Indian War

THE PERIOD OF THE REVOLUTION

1765 The Stamp Act
1770 The Boston Massacre
1773 The Boston Tea-Party
1774 The Port of Boston closed
     The First Continental Congress

1775–83 Revolutionary War
1776 Declaration of Independence
1787 The Constitutional Convention
1788 The Constitution adopted

THE NATIONAL PERIOD

1789–97 Washington's administrations
1793 Invention of the cotton gin
1800 Washington made the national capital
1801–5 War with Tripoli
1803 The Louisiana Purchase
1804–6 The Lewis and Clarke expedition to the Pacific Coast
1812–14 War with England
1820 The Missouri Compromise
1823 The Formulation of the Monroe Doctrine
1830 The first steam railroad in America

1844 The first electric telegraph in America
1845 The annexation of Texas
1846–47 The Mexican War
1848 Discovery of gold in California
1850 The Fugitive Slave Law
1858 The first Atlantic cable
1861–65 The Civil War
1869 A railroad completed to the Pacific
1886 Organization of the American Federation of Labor
1887 The Interstate Commerce Law
1890 The Anti-Trust Law

1898 The Spanish-American War

1914 The Panama Canal finished

1917 The United States entered the World War

1917 Prohibition amendment ratified; repealed, 1933

1918 World War ended

1919 Ratification of Versailles Treaty, including adherence to the League of Nations, defeated

1920 Woman Suffrage amendment ratified

1922 Teapot Dome oil scandal

1924 Nine Power Pact ratified

1929 Kellogg-Briand Anti-War Treaty
Panic on stock exchange ends five-year "boom"

1933 Bank crisis; "the depression"

1935 Social Security Act

1936 Unemployment Insurance Act
Inter-American Neutrality Convention

1938 Reciprocal trade agreement with the British Empire
Pan-American Conference at Lima adopted a declaration of "the solidarity of America" and of "American principles" in international relations

1939 The President invites Hitler and Mussolini to guarantee the integrity of small European nations
King George and Queen Elizabeth visit the United States
First commercial passenger airplane flight to Europe

1940 Franklin D. Roosevelt elected to a third term

1941 The President declares America to be "the arsenal of democracy"
Lease-Lend Act for aid to Great Britain and her Allies

II. ENGLISH LITERATURE

THE ELIZABETHAN AGE, 1558–1642

1599 Shakspere (1564–1616): *Julius Caesar*

1603 Jonson (d. 1637): *Sejanus*
Shakspere: *Hamlet*

1605 Shakspere: *King Lear*

1606 Shakspere: *Macbeth*

1608 Beaumont and Fletcher: *Philaster*

1610 Jonson: *The Alchemist*

1610–11 Shakspere: *The Tempest*

1611 The King James Version of the Bible

1612 Bacon (1561–1626): *Essays*, second edition

1620 Bacon: *Novum Organum*

1623 Shakspere: *Comedies, Histories, and Tragedies* (the First Folio)

1630 Quarles: *Divine Poems*

1631 Herbert: *The Temple*

1634 Milton (1608–74): *Comus*

1635 Quarles: *Emblems*

1638 Milton: *Lycidas*

THE PURITAN PERIOD, 1642–1660

1644 Milton: *Areopagitica*
1645 Milton: *Poems*
     Waller: *Poems*
1648 Herrick (d. 1674): *Hesperides*

1650 Baxter: *The Saints' Everlasting Rest*
     Taylor: *Holy Living*
1653 Walton: *The Compleat Angler*

THE PERIOD OF THE RESTORATION, 1660–1700

1660 Dryden (1631–1700): *Astræa Redux*
1663 Butler: *Hudibras*, Part I
1666 Bunyan (d. 1688): *Grace Abounding to the Chief of Sinners*
1667 Dryden: *Annus Mirabilis*
     Milton: *Paradise Lost*
1670 Dryden: *The Conquest of Granada*
1671 Milton: *Paradise Regained, Samson Agonistes*
1672 Dryden: *Marriage à la Mode*

1678 Bunyan: *The Pilgrim's Progress*
     Dryden: *All for Love*
1681 Dryden: *Absalom and Achitophel*
1682 Otway: *Venice Preserved*
1687 Dryden: *The Hind and the Panther*
1690 Locke: *Essay concerning the Human Understanding*
1695 Congreve: *Love for Love*
1698 Collier: *A Short View of the Immorality and Profaneness of the English Stage*

THE AGE OF POPE, 1700–1744

1700 Congreve: *The Way of the World*
1702 Defoe (d. 1731): *The Shortest Way with the Dissenters*
1704 Swift (d. 1745): *A Tale of a Tub*
1707 Farquhar: *The Beaux' Stratagem*
1709 Pope (1688–1744): *Pastorals*
     Steele and Addison: *The Tatler;* ended January, 1711
1711 Steele and Addison: *The Spectator;* ended December, 1712
1712 Pope: *The Rape of the Lock*
1713 Pope: *Windsor Forest*
1715 Defoe: *An Appeal to Honour and Justice*
     Pope: Translation of the *Iliad*
1719 Defoe: *Robinson Crusoe*

1720 Watts: *Divine and Moral Songs*
1721 Ramsay: *Poems*
1722 Defoe: *A Journal of the Plague Year*
     Steele: *The Conscious Lovers*
1724 Defoe: *Roxana*
1726 Swift: *Gulliver's Travels*
     Thomson (d. 1748): *Winter*
1728 Pope: *The Dunciad*
1731 Lillo: *George Barnwell*
1732 Pope: *Essay on Man*
1738 Johnson (1709–84): *London*
1740 Richardson (d. 1761): *Pamela*
1742 Fielding (1707–54): *Joseph Andrews*
     Young: *Night Thoughts*
1743 Blair: *The Grave*

THE AGE OF JOHNSON, 1744–1798

1744 Akenside: *The Pleasures of the Imagination*

1746 Collins (d. 1759): *Odes*

1747 Gray (d. 1771): *Ode on a Distant Prospect of Eton College*

1748 Richardson: *Clarissa Harlowe*
Smollett (d. 1771): *Roderick Random*

1749 Fielding: *Tom Jones*

1751 Gray: *Elegy Written in a Country Churchyard*

1755 Johnson: *Rasselas*
Sterne (d. 1768): *Tristram Shandy*, Vols. I, II

1761 Churchill: *Rosciad*

1762 Macpherson: *The Poems of Ossian*

1764 Walpole (d. 1797): *The Castle of Otranto*

1765 Percy: *Reliques of Ancient English Poetry*

1766 Goldsmith (d. 1774): *The Vicar of Wakefield*

1768 Gray: *Poems*

1770 Goldsmith: *The Deserted Village*

1773 Goldsmith: *She Stoops To Conquer*

1775 Burke (d. 1797): *On Conciliation with the Colonies*
Sheridan: *The Rivals*

1776 Gibbon: *History of the Decline and Fall of the Roman Empire*, Vol. I

1778 Burney: *Evelina*

1779 Johnson: *Lives of the Poets*

1783 Crabbe: *The Village*

1784 Beckford: *Vathek*

1785 Cowper: *The Task*

1786 Burns (1759–96): *Poems Chiefly in the Scottish Dialect*

1789 Burke: *Reflections on the Revolution in France*

1791 Boswell: *The Life of Samuel Johnson*

1793 Godwin (d. 1836): *An Inquiry concerning Political Justice*

1794 Godwin: *Caleb Williams*
Radcliffe: *Mysteries of Udolpho*

THE ROMANTIC PERIOD, 1798–1832

1798 Wordsworth (1770–1850) and Coleridge (1772–1834): *Lyrical Ballads*

1799 Campbell: *The Pleasures of Hope*

1801 Southey (d. 1842): *Thalaba, the Destroyer*

1805 Scott (1771–1832): *The Lay of the Last Minstrel*

1807 Wordsworth: *Poems*

1808 Scott: *Marmion*

1809 Campbell: *Gertrude of Wyoming*

1810 Scott: *The Lady of the Lake*

1811 Austen (d. 1817): *Sense and Sensibility*

1812 Byron (1788–1824): *Childe Harold's Pilgrimage*, Cantos 1 and 2

1814 Byron: *The Corsair, Lara*
Scott: *Waverley*

1815 Wordsworth: *Poems*

1816 Coleridge: *Cristabel*
Shelley (d. 1822): *Alastor*

1817 Keats (d. 1821): *Poems*

1819 Byron: *Don Juan*, Cantos 1 and 2

1820 Keats: *Poems*
Scott: *Ivanhoe*
Shelley: *Prometheus Unbound*
1821 De Quincey (d. 1859): *Confessions of an English Opium Eater*

1821 Hazlitt (d. 1830): *Table Talk*
1823 Lamb (d. 1834): *Essays of Elia*
Scott: *Quentin Durward*
1830 Tennyson (1809–92): *Poems Chiefly Lyrical*

Victorian Period, 1832–1892

1833 Browning (1812–89): *Pauline*
Tennyson: *Poems*
1836–37 Dickens (1812–70): *Pickwick Papers*
1837 Carlyle (d. 1881): *The French Revolution*
1841 Carlyle: *Heroes and Hero-Worship*
1842 Browning: *Dramatic Lyrics*
Tennyson: *Poems*
1843 Dickens: *Martin Chuzzelwit*
Macaulay (d. 1859): *Essays*
1844 E. B. Browning: *Poems*
1847 C. Brontë: *Jane Eyre*
1847–48 Thackeray (1811–63): *Vanity Fair*
1848 Arnold (d. 1888): *The Strayed Reveller*
1849–50 Dickens: *David Copperfield*
Thackeray: *Pendennis*
1850 Tennyson: *In Memoriam*
1851 E. B. Browning: *Casa Guidi Windows*
1852 Thackeray: *Henry Esmond*
1855 Browning: *Men and Women*
Kingsley: *Westward Ho!*
1857 Trollope: *Barchester Towers*
1858 Morris: *The Defense of Guinevere*
Tennyson: *Idylls of the King*
1859 Darwin: *Origin of Species*
G. Eliot (d. 1880): *Adam Bede*
1860 Dickens: *Great Expectations*

1861 Reade: *The Cloister and the Hearth*
1864 Newman (d. 1890): *Apologia pro Vita Sua*
Swinburne (d. 1909): *Atalanta in Calydon*
1865 Meredith (d. 1909): *Rhoda Fleming*
1866 G. Eliot: *Felix Holt*
Swinburne: *Poems and Ballads*
1868 Browning: *The Ring and the Book*
Morris: *The Earthly Paradise* begun
1869 Arnold: *Culture and Anarchy*
1870 Rossetti (d. 1882): *Poems*
1871 Swinburne: *Songs before Sunrise*
1872 Hardy: *Under the Greenwood Tree*
1873 Arnold: *Literature and Dogma*
Pater (d. 1894): *Studies in the History of the Renaissance*
1876 Morris: *Sigurd the Volsung*
1878 Hardy: *The Return of the Native*
1879 Browning: *Dramatic Idyls*
Meredith: *The Egoist*
1881 Rossetti: *Ballads and Sonnets*
Swinburne: *Mary Stuart*
1883 Browning: *Jocoseria*
Stevenson (d. 1894): *Treasure Island*
1884 Tennyson: *Becket*
1885 Tennyson: *Tiresias and Other Poems*
1888 Kipling: *Plain Tales from the Hills*

1889 Browning: *Asolando*
Pater: *Appreciations*
Tennyson: *Demeter and Other Poems*
1890 Watson: *Wordsworth's Grave*
1891 Barrie: *The Little Minister*

1891 Doyle (d. 1930): *The Adventures of Sherlock Holmes*
Hardy: *Tess of the D'Urbervilles*
1892 Kipling: *Barrack-Room Ballads*
Tennyson: *The Death of Œnone and Other Poems*

POST-VICTORIAN AUTHORS

1893 Pinero: *The Second Mrs. Tanqueray*
1894 Kipling (d. 1936): *The Jungle Book*
Moore: *Esther Waters*
Yeats: *The Land of Heart's Desire*
1895 Wells: *The Time Machine*
1896 Barrie (d. 1937): *Sentimental Tommy*
Hardy: *Jude the Obscure*
1897 Conrad (d. 1924): *The Nigger of the "Narcissus"*
1898 Hewlett (d. 1923): *The Forest Lovers*
Phillpotts: *Children of the Mist*
Shaw: *Plays, Pleasant and Unpleasant*
1900 Conrad: *Lord Jim*
Jones (d. 1929): *Mrs. Dane's Defence*
1901 Kipling: *Kim*
1902 Masefield: *Saltwater Ballads*
1904 Barrie: *Peter Pan*
Hardy (d. 1922): *The Dynasts*, Part I
1906 Galsworthy: *The Man of Property*
Hudson (d. 1922): *A Crystal Age*
1907 Bottomley: *Chambers of Imagery*
1908 Bennett (d. 1931): *The Old Wives' Tale*
Chesterton (d. 1936): *Orthodoxy*
Noyes: *Drake*

1909 Kipling: *Actions and Reactions*
Masefield: *The Tragedy of Nan*
1910 Galsworthy (d. 1933): *Justice*
Wells: *The History of Mr. Polly*
1911 Masefield: *The Everlasting Mercy*
Shaw: *Fanny's First Play*
1912 Stephens: *The Crock of Gold*
1913 Cannan: *Round the Corner*
Galsworthy: *The Dark Flower*
Mackenzie: *Sinister Street*, Vol. I
1914 Conrad: *Chance*
Dunsany: *Five Plays*
1915 Brooke (d. 1915): *Collected Poems*
1916 Sidgwick: *Hatchways*
Walpole: *The Dark Forest*
Wells: *Mr. Britling Sees It Through*
1917 Sassoon: *The Old Huntsman*
Swinnerton: *Nocturne*
1918 Barrie: *Echoes of the War* (Plays)
Drinkwater: *Abraham Lincoln*
1920 Bottomley: *King Lear's Wife and Other Plays*
Masefield: *Reynard the Fox*
Shaw: *Back to Methusaleh*
1921 Beerbohm: *And Even Now*
Maugham: *The Circle*
1922 Galsworthy: *The Forsyte Saga*
Joyce: *Ulysses*
Housman: *Last Poems*
"K. Mansfield": *The Garden Party*

1923 Ellis: *The Dance of Life*
Lawrence: *The Captain's Doll*
Macaulay: *Told by an Idiot*
Maugham: *Our Betters*
Shaw: *Saint Joan*

1924 Forster: *A Passage to India*
Guedalla: *A Gallery*
Kennedy: *The Constant Nymph*
Masefield: *Sard Harker*

1925 Blunden: *Masks of Time*
Coward: *Three Plays*
V. Woolf (d. 1941): *Mrs. Dalloway*

1926 Buchan: *The Dancing Floor*
Lawrence: *The Plumed Serpent*
O'Casey: *The Plough and the Stars*

1927 "E. M. Delafield": *The Way Things Are*
Maugham: *The Letter*

1928 A. Huxley: *Point Counter Point*
Masefield: *The Coming of Christ*
L. Strachey: *Elizabeth and Essex*

1929 Priestley: *The Good Companions*

1930 Auden: *Poems*
Maugham: *Cakes and Ale*
V. Sackville-West: *The Edwardians*

1931 Buchan: *The Blanket of the Dark*
Coward: *Cavalcade*
"E. M. Delafield": *The Provincial Lady*

1932 Bentley: *Inheritance*
A. Huxley: *Brave New World*

1933 Brittain: *Testament of Youth*
Wells: *The Shape of Things To Come*

1934 Bottome: *Private Worlds*
S. Gibbons: *Cold Comfort Farm*
Sayers: *The Nine Tailors*

1935 Spender: *Vienna*
F. B. Young: *White Ladies*

1936 Priestley: *They Walk in the City*

1937 Cronin: *The Citadel*

1938 D. Du Maurier: *Rebecca*

1940 Masefield: *Basilissa*
Priestley: *Let the People Sing*

INDEXES

INDEX OF AUTHORS

INDEX OF SUBJECTS